DEVIL'S ADVOCATE

DEVIL'S ADVOCATES is a series of books devoted to exploring the classics of horror cinema. Contributors to the series come from the fields of teaching, academia, journalism and fiction, but all have one thing in common: a passion for the horror film and a desire to share it with the widest possible audience.

'The admirable Devil's Advocates series is not only essential – and fun – reading for the serious horror fan but should be set texts on any genre course.'
Dr Ian Hunter, Reader in Film Studies, De Montfort University, Leicester

'Auteur Publishing's new Devil's Advocates critiques on individual titles... offer bracingly fresh perspectives from passionate writers. The series will perfectly complement the BFI archive volumes.' **Christopher Fowler,** *Independent on Sunday*

'Devil's Advocates has proven itself more than capable of producing impassioned, intelligent analyses of genre cinema... quickly becoming the go-to guys for intelligent, easily digestible film criticism.' *Horror Talk.com*

'Auteur Publishing continue the good work of giving serious critical attention to significant horror films.' *Black Static*

 DevilsAdvocatesbooks

DevilsAdBooks

ALSO AVAILABLE IN THIS SERIES

FORTHCOMING

DEVIL'S ADVOCATES

REPULSION

JEREMY CARR

Acknowledgements

To my parents. Thanks for everything.

First published in 2021 by
Auteur, an imprint of
Liverpool University Press,
4 Cambridge Street,
Liverpool
L69 7ZU

Series design: Nikki Hamlett at Cassels Design
Set by Cassels Design
Printed and bound by CPI Group (UK) Ltd, Croydon CR0 4YY

British Library Cataloguing-in-Publication Data
A catalogue record for this book is available from the British Library

ISBN paperback: 978-1-80085-933-3
ISBN hardback: 978-1-80085-932-6
ISBN epub: 978-1-80085-811-4
ISBN PDF: 978-1-80085-851-0

CONTENTS

INTRODUCTION

Roman Polanski probably wouldn't care for much of what is contained in this book. Or, at least he probably wouldn't agree with it. For one thing, Polanski has, throughout his career, been reluctant to entertain the prescribed deeper motives of his work, the latent meanings and intentions of his narratives, the self-conscious complexities of his formal choices or the interpretations of his thematic tendencies. While remaining remarkably candid about the traumatic aspects of his past as well as his current worldview, he has, at the same time, also resisted the offer to ascribe in his filmography any undue ingredients derivative of his childhood and, later, the other distressing events that have shaped his life and subsequent career. And yet, as has often been the case in texts about Polanski and his films, these features and this general critical inclination are nearly unavoidable. The markers are too obvious to be ignored; the connections are too prescient to be dismissed.

What is particularly relevant in this regard, and with this study especially, is how these elements correspond to Polanski's varied explorations into the horror genre. Born August 18, 1933 in France, but tragically relocated to the disquiet of 1936 Poland, on the cusp of World War II, Polanski was besieged from a young age by looming Nazism, an oppressive ghetto, the threat of potential concentration camp incarceration and, most definitive and distressing of all, lurking death itself. He endured an extended period of panicked solitude and a first-hand encounter with the true terrors of mankind. Surviving and thriving nevertheless, his preliminary work in radio and theater, entering both avenues of expression as a child, led to his enrollment in the National Film School in Lodz, Poland, and the creation of several short films, many of which (*Teeth Smile* and *Murder*, both from 1957, and *The Lamp*, from 1959) introduce motifs common to Polanski's succeeding output: inhibiting confines, voyeurism, the surrealistic expression of everyday occurrences and the sinister potency of inanimate objects. His debut feature, *Knife in the Water* (1962), a boldly perilous thriller released in Poland when he was just 28 years old, garnered Polanski widespread acclaim and notoriety, including a 1964 Oscar nomination for Best Foreign Language Film. But as he struggled to begin his next proposed film, initially titled 'If Katelbach Comes,' Polanski was instead engaged by the Compton Group, a British production company largely known for exploitation and soft porn fare and currently in search of horror movie fodder—especially if it could conceivably come from an internationally renowned filmmaker. The result was *Repulsion* (1965), written by Polanski and Gérard Brach, their first of eight collaborations. Starring Catherine Deneuve, it became a film that would encompass an array of the aforementioned interests—narrative, visual and thematic—at once alluding to Polanski's prior life and work, previewing the same aspects in his future endeavors and demonstrating numerous defining characteristics of the horror genre generally.

Despite his reticence to connect the biographical-to-artistic dots, the first words of Polanski's 1984 autobiography, *Roman*, seem to tease the suitability. 'For as far back as I can remember,' he wrote, 'the line between fantasy and reality has been hopelessly blurred' (1985: 1). As with the torment suffered by Deneuve's demure beautician, Carol Ledoux, and as a theme manifest in many of his most affecting films, *Repulsion* among them, there has been in Polanski's own life a significant overlap between the real world and an imaginary one, a psychological methodology, conscious or not, that has served the filmmaker well. Spending time in a largely unfurnished Warsaw apartment as a young boy, living his nights and most days in a cramped, hindering basement, Polanski's childhood was marred by terrified crowds, frightening noises, stifling heat and an omnipresent paranoia concerning prospective German invasion at any moment. Contained by a walled-in ghetto and even later as he managed to flee, Polanski was surrounded by violence. But as life went on, he, his surviving family (his mother was murdered at Auschwitz) and many of those around him were simultaneously living mundane moments of routine existence, merged and intersecting with these sporadic moments of terror. Exposed to the ugly truths about humanity—before, during and after the war—it would seem inevitable, then, that such palpable horrors would seep into his creative imagination, soon to be apparent in his impending works of art.

The processing of such material, according to some sources, began as early as Polanski's days in draft school. 'During an occasional exercise in a life class,' one of his teachers recalled, Polanski 'would grotesquely distort the subject so that it was not only unidentifiable but fiendishly macabre.' Commenting in 1968, the educator noted how he took 'a certain childish glee in turning what was supposed to be a still life of apples, pears and flowers into a collection of gruesome, surrealistic animals, crushed and gushing with blood. [...] or a nude into a human figure without skin, just a collection of bloody organs spilling like Dali watches into a puddle of scarlet ooze, with figures of strange, emaciated dogs lapping up the blood' (Kiernan, 1980: 82). Thereafter enrolling in film school, in 1954, after two rejections the year prior, Polanski turned this budding preoccupation to the realm of cinematic horror and suspense. *Murder*, his first completed short film, is, according to Barbara Leaming, 'a reverie of violence, but it is less the act of violence than the watching of it that fascinate the director' (1981: 31). The early voyeuristic propensity was not just appreciably applicable to the shock of this particular film's depicted incident, exhibiting a fascination with the process of looking and, while doing so, not wanting to be drawn to the actual horror of the act itself, but is a central motif running throughout the horror genre, including Polanski's own diverse entries.

Running just two minutes, *Murder* is a brief exposition with an unassuming victim, the wielding of a straight razor, a wave of initial panic, a struggle, ensuing bloodshed and the downbeat aftermath. On the surface, these features and Polanski's attention to brutality and black-gloved stealth seem to introduce fundamental facets of the Giallo, which would emerge in the coming years as a very Polanski-esque horror/thriller subgenre. More specifically, though, they also set the stage for Polanski's own body of work (*Repulsion* most of all). 'Not to overanalyze,' writes James Greenberg, alluding to that unavoidable, albeit reticent tendency to delve deep into Polanski's oeuvre, 'it is instructive to see what was on the twenty-four-year-old director's mind—murder and bloodletting. [...] The creepiness of the setting and terror of the victim in the instant before he is killed is intense' (2013: 23). *The Lamp*, which Polanski made in 1959, continued the trend, with its creation and arrangement of inherently unnerving dolls rendered effectively tattered and increasingly unpleasant to evoke an impressive sense of the uncanny. 'In a real Polanski touch,' Greenberg observes, 'the man picks up a realistic looking pair of eyeballs from a table of eyeballs and puts them in place through the top of the doll's head. Other disembodied doll parts are strewn about the room. [...] One thing Polanski proves here that remained with him for the rest of his career is that what you see all depends on how you look at it' (2013: 27). Again, there is the horrific blend of unsettling imagery, presented with barefaced concentration, and the subjective reading of said content, the full, disconcerting impact of which is derived primarily from one's unique point of view. These touches are pervasive in Polanski's earliest work, from *Teeth Smile*, with its own voyeuristic, skulking menace, to *Two Men and a Wardrobe*, an ostensibly comic 1958 short that begins with the incongruous image of two men emerging from the sea, lugging a cupboard into restaurants and elsewhere, but descends into cruelty as young boys (young actor Polanski among them) participate in assorted acts of brutality. The next year, the stolid entrapment and despair of *When Angels Fall* (1959), with its central character being an elderly, lowly lavatory attendant, is shown to 'epitomize vacuity, drudgery, monotony,' in Polanski's words (1985: 139), doing so by integrating images of confinement, anguish and squalor.

After the phenomenal global success of *Knife in the Water*, which assimilates and accentuates many of these same attributes, Polanski endeavored to make 'If Katelbach Comes' as his second feature. But when that project stalled, as noted above, Polanski and producer Gene Gutowski, also a Polish survivor of World War II's atrocities, set their sights on a commercial genre release, to gain further traction in the industry and to secure the necessary financial backing for Polanski's more desired follow-up. After Gutowski initially approached Hammer Film Productions, then the preeminent studio for horror cinema in England, if not the world, the duo turned to the Compton Group, which, according to Polanski, 'rejoiced in a high-sounding name'—that is, his own. The director notes: 'Everything seemed to suggest that it was a major entertainment and communications conglomerate. Actually it owed its existence and main revenue to a small, seedy SoHo establishment called the Compton cinema club, which showed what currently passed in London for porno movies' (1985: 195). Looking to gain a degree of credibility by adding a dose of artiness and celebrity to their sexually-charged, relatively low-brow library, Compton wanted horror, and they wanted it from the likes of Roman Polanski.

Partly inspired by a shared friend of Polanski and Brach's, a friend who was, according to Polanski, 'simultaneously attracted to and repelled by sex as well as prone to sudden, unpredictable bouts of violence' (1985: 198), *Repulsion*, as this Compton project became known, was also likely informed by Polanski's brief relationship with a young actress named Sonya. Dubbed 'crazy' (Kiernan, 1980: 123) by a former Lodz student and friend of Polanski's, the young lady, it seems, stabbed two prior boyfriends, attempted the same with Polanski and 'was finally carted off to a mental ward and nothing was heard of her again.' According to the friend, Sonya 'left quite an impression on Roman. Whenever I've

Fig. 1. Adding artiness to low-budget horror.

seen the films he's made, the ones with the crazy women, like *Repulsion*, I think of his experience with her' (Kiernan, 1980: 124). Working from a 12-page outline for a horror feature—its script form titled *Lovelihead*, then *The Edge of Darkness*, then, ultimately, *Repulsion*—the final screenplay was written by Polanski and Brach over the course of 17 days spent in Paris (adaptation and additional dialogue would be credited to David Stone). Writing the film to ensure the financing from Michael Klinger and Tony Tenser, owners of the Compton Group, Polanski acknowledged:

> To hook them, the screenplay had to be unmistakably horrific; they were uninterested in any other kind of film. Anything too sophisticated would have scared them off, so the plot [...] included bloodcurdling scenes that verged on horror film clichés. Any originality we achieved would have to come through in our telling of the story, which we wanted to make a realistic and psychologically credible as we could (1985: 197).

'Having a good idea of the kind of fear we wished to convey,' Polanski recalled, 'we sought inspiration from situations familiar to us' (1985: 197). This familiarity, as it had in his student films, tended to center on an appreciation of how elements of ordinary reality could suddenly transform, by means of cinematic execution or the perceived vantage of an ill-equipped victim or voyeur, into something quite ominous indeed. 'Most people,' Polanski writes, 'at one time or another, have experienced an irrational dread of some sinister unseen presence in their home. An unremembered rearrangement of furniture, a creaking floorboard, a picture falling off the wall—anything can trigger this sensation' (1985: 197). Secondarily, but a 'no less important theme' for the writer-director, was the 'lack of awareness of those who live with the mentally disturbed, familiarity having blunted their perception of the abnormal' (1985: 198). There is, then as it would often be in Polanski's work, the horror that emerges from something apparently customary and the (mis)perception of what lies beneath.

Though with a firm grasp of what could plausibly make a successful horror film, augmenting the superficial qualities of the genre with these psychological enhancements, Polanski was nevertheless of two minds about the prospect of conventional genre filmmaking. He seems to reluctantly acknowledge that the genesis for *Repulsion* was because he wanted to make a horror film in the first place, stating, 'Even though during the film's production things changed, the initial idea was to make a horror film. I'd like to deny this but it just wouldn't be true' (Cronin, 2005: 43). Yet he also said in 1988, speaking to Michel Perez following the release of *Frantic* that same year, the reason he routinely makes genre films is because he 'really love[s] cinema, and genre is what cinema is all about' (Cronin, 2005: 124). So, while Polanski considered genre to be the crux of what defines cinema, there appeared to be something about horror that made it less than substantial to his way of thinking (perhaps due to lackluster efforts seen at film school or as a young man). In any event, although he regarded *Repulsion* as a means to an end—getting 'Katelbach' off the ground—that did not mean Polanski wasn't going to give his all to the project. 'In order to justify the making of *Repulsion* to myself,' he wrote, again appearing to downplay or denigrate its status, a result of indifferent genre precepts or simply his desire to move forward with 'Katelbach,' 'I had to give it a significance that would set it head and shoulders above the average horror movie. This meant that I had to make the picture on my own terms. The only way I could upgrade it was by injecting the kind of quality that was time-consuming and, thus, more expensive than Compton had bargained for' (1985: 205).

The film had, in Polanski's view, been 'unrealistically budgeted on the low side, and [he] was taking longer to complete it than they had expected' (1985: 205). Complete it he did, though, and *Repulsion* debuted at the May 19, 1965 Cannes Film Festival before receiving theatrical releases internationally, and it would win the top prize, the

Silver Bear, at the 1965 Berlin Film Festival, an award Klinger picked up himself and never gave to Polanski. *Repulsion* was a box office success in the United States and was promptly appreciated for its depiction of mental illness. According to Polanski, psychiatrist Dr. Steven Blake attended an early screening of the picture, essentially to consult on its handling of sex and violence and whether or not any aspect seemed unnecessary or objectionable, and based in part on his evaluation, it was decided to leave everything intact. Blake, he writes, declared Carol a 'clinically accurate study of a homicidal schizophrenic.' Still, Polanski conceded, 'it embarrassed me to have to admit that we'd simply used our imagination' (1985: 211). Curiously, however, suggesting professional involvement from the very beginning, Davide Caputo explains in his *Polanski and Perception: The Psychology of Seeing and the Cinema of Roman Polanski* that a British Board of Film Classification Examiner's Report' refers to Dr. Stephen *Black* (not Blake, as Polanski calls him in his autobiography), who was 'enlisted to serve as consultant for the project during the script phase.' Blake apparently considered the script to be '"very accurate in psychiatric terms"' but 'strongly recommended [...] that some amendments should be made in order to ensure the film was not a danger to psychotics' (2012: 82).

Fig. 2. A 'clinically accurate study of a homicidal schizophrenic.'

Whatever his intentions, whatever his early thoughts on the genre, and in no small part due to the positive reception of *Repulsion* further buoyed by subsequent features like *The Fearless Vampire Killers* (1967), *Rosemary's Baby* (1968) and *The Tenant* (1976), Polanski's name became one synonymous with horror. But it has proved to be a complicated, multifaceted association, one often linked to his problematic life story. The work that actually appears on screen, as well as the frequently corresponding perceptions of his own character, a correlation seen in the very titles of biographies and critical studies about Polanski and his films, tend to draw rather blatant parallels between aspects of Polanski's true self and his ostensive persona. A sampling of phrasing includes the tagline ascribed to Thomas Kiernan's 1980 Polanski biography—'Fascinating. Evil. Corrupt. A cinema genius.'—and the subtitle of Leaming's text—'The Filmmaker as Voyeur'—as well as her description of Polanski as a 'virtuoso of violence' (1985: 11). Polanski himself acknowledged that people habitually saw him as an 'evil, profligate dwarf' (Greenberg, 2013: 11). The malice and violence aligned with this perception is, not surprisingly, far more nuanced than the media-driven sensationalism and the consequently shallow slant of his public and private personality. Likewise, his films are far more complex than their depicted acts of ferocity and terror, to the point where his horror features are in fact quite more than what the genre requires, at minimum, while his films existing outside the conventions of the genre often incorporate many of its essential characteristics. This is particularly the case when it comes to violence; not just the violence typically associated with horror (of which there is actually very little in his filmography), but a violence that derives from psychological, sexual and emotional sources. 'Polanski's films have never been merely about violence,' notes Leaming:

> Like Hitchcock, he is fascinated by the enigma of violence observed, the special allure of base acts. But Polanski goes beyond Hitchcock, whose gory masterpieces are made palatable by the ironic distance of the rotund family man, a director with an impeccable personal life. More is at stake with Polanski, whose own violent life and times—from Hitler to the Manson "family"—form the subtext of his cinema (1981: 11).

Forgetting what we now know to the be the disturbing truth about Hitchcock's 'impeccable personal life'—indeed, in light of recent revelations, a similar study of the venerable master's own personal-professional overlap would yield fascinating results—Leaming does point to a pivotal area concerning Polanski's depiction of horrific deeds, namely how his biographical touchstones often appear to inform his work and, especially around the time of the Manson murders, vice-versa: details of the August 9, 1969 slaying of Polanski's pregnant wife, Sharon Tate, along with four friends, were warped in the media to include erroneous elements of occultism and devil worship, elements not coincidentally associated with similar content in *Rosemary's Baby*, released the year prior.

Drawing inspiration from Polanski's background as evidence to the troubling nature of his work, many, like Herbert J. Eagle, point to the 'traumatic years of [Polanski's] youth,' 'years [that] provided him with his characteristic view of the world and of the ubiquity of evil' (Orr/Ostrowska, 2006: 40). Others, meanwhile, are prone to question the apparent fascination based on such trauma. 'Why would a man who had witnessed so much genuine horror in actual life be so enamored of ersatz abjection?' asks David Ehrenstein. 'Clearly he found in celluloid fantasy a way of dealing with the residual pain of concrete reality' (2012: 19). Whatever the reason, and they need not be mutually exclusive, the fact, as James Morrison states, 'that horror is the cinematic genre with which Roman Polanski has been most closely identified is something of an accident of history' (2007: 18). True enough. Of his more than twenty features, only five are generally regarded as 'traditional' horror films: *Repulsion*, *Rosemary's Baby*, *The Tenant*, *The Ninth Gate* (1999) and *The Fearless Vampire Killers*, the latter two of which Morrison says are 'actually horror burlesque' (2007: 18). As far as *Repulsion* is concerned, even it manages to transcend or even bypass some of the more conventional aspects of the genre. 'For all its horrific imagery,' states Morrison, it 'has none of the supernatural trappings that purist of the form demand' (2007: 18). Yet horror it most certainly is.

Polanski's brand of horror, and a primary reason why so much of his work seems to fall within the broad definition of the genre, or at least how it incorporates discerning elements of the genre into films otherwise removed from the form, extends beyond the cliched images and incidents of genre cinema itself and reaches a more profound, extensive and comprehensive view of a world consumed by tangible, pervasive fear. Comments Tony McKibbin, 'If we think of Polanski in relation to horror, horror as a word reflecting a problem with the world rather than a genre expectation, then we can incorporate almost all of his work within the feeling of horror without worrying too much about genre pedants' (Orr/Ostrowska, 2006: 60). That expressive, deep-seated feeling, the concept of an inherent malevolence and the sensation of knowing something isn't as it should be, is at the heart of many horror films, as an unexplained phenomenon develops from some malicious force, supernatural or otherwise, but it equally applies to the thriller, arguably Polanski's more prominent genre home. From this sense of subversive alarm, Morrison writes, Polanski's 'treatment of isolation just as often concerns escapism—a conscious effort to remove oneself from the social sphere—as it does abjection' (2007: 12). To this end, per Helena Goscilo, Polanski has emerged as 'a director who conceives of everyday life as banal horror' (Orr/Ostrowska, 2006: 23), which is precisely where the horror of *Repulsion* resides. And from that, his approach to horror transcends the trivial. He is, accordingly, in the words of McKibbin, 'a great filmmaker not of generic horror but existential, even ontological horror' (Orr/Ostrowska, 2006: 61). Altogether, the universally ordinary presence of something horrific became an overriding factor in how Polanski's cinema evolved, and why the horror genre came to be perhaps the dominant form associated with his work, accurately or not. For Polanski, though, this frequent return to horror stems from far less serious reasoning: 'I like all horror films,' he stated. 'They make me laugh like crazy' (Ehrenstein, 2012: 19).

Chapter 1: ISOLATION AND ENTRAPMENT

In *Repulsion*, Carol Ledoux, a Belgian manicurist living in London's South Kensington district with her older sister Helen (Yvonne Furneaux), is initially and primarily troubled by her sister's married boyfriend, Michael (Ian Hendry), who frequently stays overnight in their apartment. As disturbed as she is by his presence, however, she is further tormented by the couple's absence when they leave for a nearly two-week Italian vacation. Carol is left to contend with her work, with the generally genial flirtations of a budding suitor, Colin (John Fraser), and the far less cordial advances of her dubious, aggressive landlord (Patrick Wymark). Worst of all, the natural anxieties extending from her introverted manner are compounded by the gestating demons of her insulated condition. As it approaches the horror formula of seclusion breeding anxiety, *Repulsion* centers on the literal and figurative isolation of Carol, her solitary position being both a catalyst and product of her failing mental fitness. Moving through life in an ominously advancing dream state, suggesting with each passing day the encroachment of something deeply and profoundly malignant, Carol shirks physical touch and reveals a foreboding cerebral sensitivity, which leads to public detachment and awkward social interaction. As she is scolded at home and at work and is overwhelmed by the threats of the outside world—genuine threats or simply perceived as such—she regresses into an emotionally opaque, inarticulate and impenetrable loneliness. The unrealized depth of her tortured temperament is amplified by her sister's holiday, leaving this fragile young woman subject to the terrors of her own solitary imaginings. This framework correlates not only to familiar horror tropes, from remote haunted houses to scenarios involving three or fewer characters in a single, inaccessible site, but to subsequent Polanski productions, from *Cul-de-sac* (1966), where two of the four main characters live a private existence largely by choice and suffer collective angst as a result, to 2002's *The Pianist*, where Polish Jew Wladyslaw Szpilman spends a considerable amount of time alone and pursued by hostile German forces.

In what would become the first installment of his so-called 'Apartment Trilogy,' which includes later films *Rosemary's Baby* and *The Tenant*, *Repulsion* commences a succession of features where the 'thematic commonalities […] chiefly, neuroses inflamed by confinement, both social and architectural—are strong enough to represent a clear through-line' (Wojtas). These are films where the limited settings magnify enduring contention and anxiety, often influenced by ambiguous external forces, directly or through a subjective interpretation, and by those who surround the main protagonists and are literally themselves partly or wholly responsible for the resulting terror. With *Repulsion*, though, it is what consumes Carol when she is alone in the apartment that most initiates the underlying torment. As it is for Rosemary and Trelkovsky, the respective protagonists/victims of *Rosemary's Baby* and *The Tenant*, the former played by Mia Farrow, the latter by Polanski himself, Carol is essentially left to contend with these threats unallied and increasingly divorced from the stability of a conventional reality. As 'one of the great filmmakers of interior horror' (Orr/Ostrowska, 2006: 51), Polanski, in this trilogy and beyond (even beyond the straightforward horror features), tends to focus on 'troubled subjects' who, writes Mark Cousins, 'move forward to tragic nemesis but never break free of the space that encloses them and recurs to haunt them' (Orr/Ostrowska, 2006: 6). So, for as much as Trelkovsky and Rosemary may seek solace or assistance elsewhere, and this they do far more than Carol even attempts, they are ultimately facing their fears and anxieties by themselves, and for each, as it is with Carol, their place of residence only fosters the continuance of these issues. In the beginning of *Repulsion*, as Tarja Laine argues, 'Carol resists the outside world by securing her personal boundaries through compulsive cleansing. Later, however, she attempts to shut out the exterior world altogether by barricading her apartment and covering all the windows' (2011). This attempt at controlled security falters, though, as transferred remnants of that exterior world manage to seep through the cracks of Carol's psyche, growing increasingly real and detrimental. It becomes that for Carol, it is the apartment which, in effect, fosters the biggest threat to her well-being, simply because it is there where she withdraws from the world and where her isolation intensifies what may, perhaps, have been alleviated elsewhere. The apartment isn't literally the facilitator, of course, as it is but a common, quite normal flat (just as Trelkovsky's and Rosemary's apartments aren't in and of themselves exceptional), but the dwelling, and Carol's retiring placement within its walls, serves the symbolic function of principal reagent. 'The flat itself starts off as merely grim and ends up as a crucible of homicidal delirium,' states Christopher Sandford, noting *Repulsion*'s similarities to *Psycho* (1960), an apt comparison given the innately spine-chilling nature of the Bates Motel in Alfred Hitchcock's film, which fuels the terror of its scenario before anything is enacted and which also assigns the source of its terror to the personification of a lonely, isolated individual with an obviously preexisting complex. Equally apt, though with as many varying traits as comparable ones, Sandford points to the Krakow ghetto, a 'very broadly similar, self-contained world with its background glimpses of the macabre and horrific' (2008: 82).

Fig. 3. An apartment with a life of its own.

A SAFE SPACE AND THE BAD HOUSE

Concerning its placement within the horror genre, *Repulsion* aligns yet diverges from the many films that position the house as an initial 'place of refuge,' where, as Barbara Creed points out, the 'monster either shelters or the victim seeks safety.' Inevitably, though, 'the situation is reversed and the house that offered a solace ultimately becomes a trap, the place where the monster is destroyed and/or the victim murdered. Almost a cliché of the contemporary horror film is the scene where the hunted locks her/ himself inside the room, trunk or cupboard and waits' (2007: 56). The notion of the apartment becoming a solace for Carol, as frightening as the outside world is, is quickly upended when it becomes clear that it is there where Carol's greatest panic resides. Yet, while the apartment only accelerates her anxiety, there is nothing precisely about the apartment itself that is a danger, nor is there an actual monstrous figure who enters the domain to cause the violence that ensues; the two who do pressure Carol by literally invading her safe space are merely ordinary men. The apartment also isn't, for example, haunted, nor do we know of any prior incident taking place there that would itself be cause for concern (unlike *The Tenant* and *Rosemary's Baby*, where those respective residences to do carry connotations of death and mystery, or even Polanski's much later *The Ghost Writer*, from 2010, where 'just as in the Apartment Trilogy, the subject to whom we are tethered finds himself occupying an abode in which traces of the former tenant still seem to "haunt" the space' [Caputo, 2012: 251]). All the same, elements in the home are more than what they seem. Rendered this way by Polanski's camera, by Deneuve's interaction within certain rooms and corridors and by the combined interpretation of their conjoining function, the home appears almost as if it is truly a malevolent force enacting its will on an unsuspecting victim at its mercy. As it impels Carol's life, the apartment takes on a life of its own, merging with and enlivening her anxieties. Comparing the film to another horror staple, McKibbin likens the internal-to-external world of *Repulsion*, where the two spheres mesh via the inner workings of a main character's mind, to Wes Craven's *A Nightmare on Elm Street* (1984), where victims are confronted by the monster, the iconic Fred Krueger (Robert Englund), in their dreams, arenas with their own peculiar, surreal and terrifying dream logic where 'the leading character [...] is merely a cipher to atmosphere; in *Repulsion* Polanski adopts atmosphere to explore the nature of exiled being' (Orr/Ostrowska, 2006: 52).

Locating *Repulsion* as something of a twist on the generic concept of the 'Bad Place' or 'Terrible House,' a 'Gothic tradition [that] serves to reinforce the ideas that the space of the contemporary house is always-already fraught, and its boundaries, like those of the body, far from fixed,' Erin Harrington notes that the bad house may also 'act as an extension of the minds, fears or personalities of those who live within it—a powerful association, given the association between women, domesticity and interior space.' In *Repulsion*, she states, 'the dissolution and decay of neurotic and sex-averse manicurist Carol's apartment mirrors her descent into psychosis' (2018: 99). As unstable and capricious as Carol herself seems to be, certainly with regards to her wavering psychological constitution, the apartment only serves to increase that potential for random change. At the same time, *Repulsion* is quite like much of Polanski's prior and subsequent work in its use of a single, cramped location to augment the gestating anxieties of human conduct. There is, for example, *Bitter Moon* (1992), where a combustible couple spends several days alone in an apartment, 'like two goldfish in a bowl,' and the claustrophobic space only engenders their already developing strain, and *Carnage* (2011), a film where the confined confrontation between four adults has comic and tense consequences emboldened by individual quirks, banal pleasantries and unbridled anger, all exacerbated by a Bunuelian inability to leave the apartment. *Knife in the Water* is perhaps the most extreme (at least the most extremely limited) example, where the picking up of a hitchhiker, itself a dangerous enough premise, adds to the ensuing tension of boat-bound recklessness, heedlessness and the fostering of 'antagonistic personalities within a confined space' (Polanski, 1985: 144), wherein Polanski's visual accent frames the friction in juxtaposition with the floating isolation and the ostensible, leisurely tranquility. Provocation and simmering resentment likewise merge in *Death and the Maiden* (1994), where its combative trio is stuck inside a house—a 'madhouse' according to Ben Kingsley's Dr. Miranda, who is rightfully disturbed by the film's turn of events (even if he brought it upon himself). While that film's anxiety is born from a very natural, very human conflict, it nevertheless mirrors *Repulsion* in that, as Kingsley rightly remarks, 'What interests Roman is the visual within the room, within the people's psyches' (Meikle, 2006: 276). There is also the unsettled, initially unexplained unease of *Cul-de-sac*, where the pervasive despondency and hostility is undercut and yet weirdly accentuated by the film's droll absurdity and its erratic personalities, forming, according to Ivan Butler, 'a kind of mad, blundering confusion, of nothing being quite right, of shifting uncertainty and logic turned upside down' (1970: 95), a logic certainly applicable to that which motivates and characterizes *Repulsion*. And of course, there are the two films that, with *Repulsion*, form the Apartment Trilogy, which as its very name suggests are essentially dependent on the innerworkings of characters encased within a single setting. 'As in *Repulsion*, Polanski uses a type of Ames Room in *The Tenant*,' according to Caputo, 'to further punctuate Trelkovsky's disturbed mental state' (2012: 154), using architecture and setting, as Leaming likewise argues, 'to provoke and reflect diseased states of mind' (1981: 150). The entire apartment complex of *The Tenant* defies the normalcy of its surface familiarity, a curious contention suggested almost instantly in the film as Trelkovsky is guided through his new home, setting the scene and opening up the potential influence of the apartment's former tenant to impact present happenings. A similar commencement is seen in *Rosemary's Baby*, only with that apartment, as the film plays out and as opposed to Carol's flat, which 'confirms and externalises her predicament even if only to herself,' the horror of Rosemary's residence will be that it 'denies her problems and forces her to internalise her sense of disturbance. [...] The matrix of terror is not, this time, the suffering mind but the tortured body' (Orr/Ostrowska, 2006: 122).

Fig. 4. The repression of inner demons.

ABJECTION AND INVASION

The term 'repulsion,' 'though related to repression,' as Lucy Fischer observes, 'implies [...] that desire is not merely stunted or postponed, but transformed into disgust or abhorrence' (Orr/Ostrowska, 2006: 77). Citing the work of Sigmund Freud, Steven Jay Schneider offers up another term related to *Repulsion*: 'unheimlich,' the name "'for everything that ought to have remained [...] secret and hidden but has come to light.'" The word's translation, 'uncanny,' Freud suggests, "'is that class of frightening things that occasion anxiety because they relate to repressed affect: something which is familiar and old-established in the mind and which has become alienated from it only through the process of repression'"(2009: 56). In this dual application of psychological conditioning, the surroundings once so familiar and unthreatening bear new significance as Carol's solitary descent increases. A degree of this is of her own doing, prompted by the willful seclusion that seems to almost invite the terror, hiding herself away in a location littered with potential triggers and reminders of what torments her in the first place. But the repression of these inner demons, reinforced by being alone, also feeds the intrinsic threat of being cut off and unable to seek help. This isolation, literally or symbolically and with its various causes, is repeated by Polanski in the cut phone lines of *Cul-de-sac*, where it is an invader who does the severing, adding outwardly-induced tension to an already remote setting, and is echoed by the isolating forces of a thunderstorm in *Death and the Maiden* and the moments where Sigourney Weaver's Paulina Escobar seeks additional seclusion within her geographically far-flung house, eating alone in a closet, for instance. There is something of a conscious detachment also seen in Polanski's *Chinatown* (1974), where private investigator J.J. Gittes (Jack Nicholson) displays a social coldness derived from the objectivity of his profession, an occupation dependent upon distanced voyeurism and emotional restraint, while, on the other hand, less of the main character's individual intent, there is what befalls Oliver Twist in Polanski's 2005 retelling of the Charles Dickens' 1837 novel, where the titular child is routinely subjected to abandonment, abuse and a reduction to solo wanderings in the countryside (traits that certainly resonate with some of the more harrowing moments in Polanski's own young life). The list continues: Ewan McGregor's unnamed author in *The Ghost Writer* is initially forced to reside in a house controlled by heightened security and made largely inaccessible on an island; Harrison Ford's luckless doctor in *Frantic* searches for his missing, likely kidnapped wife in France, all while being unable to speak the native language and wary of most everyone he encounters; Nastassja Kinski's title character in *Tess* (1979) is forced into a social solitude due to the stigmas of a prejudicial culture; and the unsuspecting tourists of *Bitter Moon* are swiftly implicated in a strange, disconcerting scenario that threatens their individual security as well as their marriage, all while temporarily residing aboard a cruise ship adrift at sea.

These characters, for the most part (certainly characters like 'good and innocent'

Oliver and someone like Carol, one of the more innocuous protagonists in any Polanski film), express a repeated Polanski refrain of bad things happening to essentially good people. They find themselves forlorn in a peculiar and hostile world, where although there is sometimes resentment to begin with (the bitter incompatibility of *Cul-de-sac*'s quarrelsome couple is established at the off), the seclusion of the narrative works in tandem with further threats by one or more vessels of outside peril. In this regard, *Repulsion* is a curious counterpoint to *The Tenant*, with its central character entering a seemingly antecedent, wicked world, while little about Carol's world appears precedingly portentous. Trelkovsky is promptly consumed, physically and psychologically, by a more cryptic terror, and as a result, eventually aligning the picture with *Repulsion*, 'The Tenant is transformed from a horror film in which an innocent is persecuted by monsters on the outside to a film that (like *Repulsion* and *Rosemary's Baby* before it) derives its lingering horror from its central character's growing isolation from the world' (Caputo, 2012: 159). It is a film where Trelkovsky's lone curiosity is tempted and his confused solitude is bent by the unusual behavior that surrounds him, where 'the everyday annoyances of city life are magnified by [his] already fragile psyche' (Greenberg, 2013: 136). With Carol as perhaps the most prominent example in Polanski's work, however, these solitary figures, withdrawn and tormented, severed from society by their own choosing or not, are at a loss in the unfamiliar terrain, alone yet surrounded by dangerous, frightening stimuli. It is what McKibbin terms, concerning Polanski's cinema at large, the 'the horror of loneliness,' where 'loneliness in such instances is not about being alone, but having absent presences invading one's existence' (Orr/Ostrowska, 2006: 56). Carol's apartment serves as something of a visualized conduit for her state of mind, exhibiting and inducing her inherent instability, further stressed by the abrupt loneliness, so that 'she defines the space of the empty flat and it defines her' (Orr/Ostrowska, 2006: 13). 'As madness accelerates, the oppressive space will expand, not contract in size,' writes Orr, and unlike *Rosemary's Baby* 'where Rosemary is increasingly paranoid but almost never alone [which isn't exactly the case, as she does spend a considerable and crucial amount of time by herself], this is a study of bleak physical solitude later echoed in *The Tenant* but which Polanski does not reprise with such grim detail until the later stages of *The Pianist*, this time with a sane hero surviving human extremes' (Orr/Ostrowska, 2006: 13).

Added in *Repulsion*, Orr continues, is 'something quite unique in Polanski's work: Carol's growing schizophrenia, heard in the magnification of ordinary sounds like the nuns laughing in the convent yard or the kitchen tap dripping and seen dramatically in the varieties of rape hallucination that all but destroy her' (Orr/Ostrowska, 2006: 13). As a French woman in London, Carol is, simply by that fact, an outsider. Even if she has the initial company of her sister and at least one kindly coworker, she struggles to adjust and is accordingly left to face many of her fears single-handedly. Emboldened by her behavior, barricading herself in the apartment, for instance, and by the way she moves around the flat, silently scanning her surroundings and the objects that populate the rooms, the increasingly daunting expanse of loneliness is shot by Polanski with little to no accompanying sound, and when there is a noise, it is often amplified, making the silent void that much more pronounced. Furthermore, what seems perfectly normal is made ominous by the way Carol simply doesn't know what to do with herself, and by the way we are left to witness this uncertainty. It is, as the eventually impeding landlord states, 'enough to drive anyone up the wall.' His additional comments—Carol being 'all alone, by the telephone,' telling her there's 'no need to be alone' and referring to her as a 'frightened little animal'—also call overt attention to her solitary confinement, the perceived vulnerability associated with this seclusion and her reticent demeanor; and coming from him as it does, with more than a touch of sexual deviance, each remark is underscored by probable risk. Viewing Carol as she stares blankly at lights and shadows and aimlessly hovers about, observing what encircles her while we observe her, one attempts to decipher this inscrutable mode of processing in an effort to interpret her glances, to discern how she herself reads the situation. The uncomfortably silent, solitary time is often held for a tactically protracted duration by Polanski, with Carol alone in the frame and only the slightest of movements or none at all. Carol has what Helena Goscilo calls a 'verbally unarticulated, paralyzing terror at ostensibly random phenomena' (Orr/Ostrowska, 2006: 31), and Polanski evokes the resulting unnerving sensation through Carol's passive blankness, which is then powerfully extended to the audience in an act of empathic, yet impenetrable, engagement. It's an example of what Schneider discusses in his essay *Towards an Aesthetics of Cinematic Horror*, quoting philosopher Robert C. Solomon on how, "'One can be horrified by that which poses no [actual] threat at all [...] In horror, one stands (or sits) aghast, frozen in place or 'glued to one's seat.' Of course, one can be frozen (or 'paralyzed') by fear, but that is when fear becomes horror. Horror involves a helplessness which fear evades'" (Prince, 2004: 136). This is what Carol feels, this utter, constricted helplessness, and it is what gives much of *Repulsion* its horrific tension, for we too are left without any recourse in terms of complete understanding, the promise of firm, communicative guidance or the feeling of spatial reprieve.

Fig. 5. Like a 'frightened little animal.'

A film like *Repulsion* becomes a perfect concoction of identifiable physical strain and subjective concern, realized in the visual arrangement of the settings and the principal characters' placement within those areas, especially when they're alone and left to the devices of their own complex, exclusively crafted conceptions. As a result, characters like Carol are, Greg Cwik states, existing 'within immersive, insular worlds woven out of the shreds of their protagonists' psyches, untethered from reason and logic' (2015). *Death and the Maiden*, one of Polanski's films which doesn't fall into the horror film category but still contains several related elements, particularly those relating to *Repulsion*, likewise plays with similar notions of curious action and intriguing inaction, resting on the perceptions and initially unstated motivations of a single female protagonist. The preliminary tone in both films is primed, slowed down, drawn out in a balanced oscillation between stagnation and shock, utterly dependent on the unreliable obscurity of one person and how she responds to her surroundings. The associative confinement in *Repulsion*, which Didier Truffot says 'spreads from the character to the film', plays a 'great part in inserting the "fantastic" into this nearly clinical case study of schizophrenia.' So, if *Repulsion* refers to the horror genre 'through its confrontation between what is real and what is supernatural, it is more concerned with a process of analysis than a set of causes.' Polanski links horror, Truffot states, 'to his heroine's increasing loneliness in order to create a subjective framework which might give a shape to a fear seen and heard, not from an external cause but from an internal one. Consequently, confinement begets insanity and is associated with obsession, a dual relation both to the image and being' (2018).

Carol's apartment, a private space within which she seeks sanctuary and has apparently achieved hitherto comfort (suggested by the way she naturally undresses upon returning home from work and by her need for domestic constancy, indicated by her dislike of household disruption), becomes, in effect, an outgrowth of her mind, a visualized indication of her psychological disorder, as genuine and as genuinely terrifying as anything more horribly concrete because for her, it is. According to Maximilian Le Cain:

> As Carol's alienation increases, the normal proportions of her flat become wildly distorted visually in reflection of her unhinged mind. The private space of the apartment is rendered even more "private" through becoming an extension of her mind. Thus the "invasions" of this intimate space, whether hallucinated or the product of a reality distorted by hallucination, all occur on the same spatial plane and with the same level of perceptual verisimilitude (Orr/Ostrowska, 2006:122).

This process puts the viewer in a privileged position to witness and interpret what is otherwise left so opaque. We are, in many ways, Carol's only constant company, an association yielding concerned compassion but leaving us unable to act on her behalf, eliciting the terror of simply perceiving and being unable to do anything about it, much in the same way Carol is herself bearing witness to her hallucinations without any obvious path toward liberation. It is as if, in the words of Tarja Laine, 'The boundaries between the self and the non-self, the subjective and the objective, the inside and the outside get dissolved in Carol's apartment.' Comparing the apartment's 'fleshy, porous walls' to a body itself, a 'lived body in the Merleau-Pontyean sense,' Laine writes 'it is both a physical (architectural) and a mental (conscious) structure with an agency and intentionality of its own, aiming to drive Carol insane. Furthermore, by inviting the spectator to participate in Carol's insanity from the inside, the film touches on the fear of our mind and body being taken over beyond our control, thereby asking us to live through the effects of agatheophobia, the fear of insanity' (2011). Particularly in light of her eventually murderous response, Polanski *has* placed us inside Carol's mind, as far as we can go and as it is incrementally informed by her psychologically constructed and manipulated space, forging a relationship with the fundamental killer or 'monster' seldom afforded in a horror film. At the same time, it's clear there is much Polanski leaves uncertain with regards to Carol's behavior, as evinced by the scenes where she is seen in awkward, inconsistent positions far from where she last appeared (this is notably the case after the perceived rape sequences). For all that we are witness to, in moments of intimacy and terror, there has been much else left unseen and unexplained by Polanski, gaps left open and to never be filled in; after one traumatic night, Carol is seen in the next sequence on the floor, aimed away from the bed, lying nude with only a strategically placed blanket to cover her, leaving unclear the unseen times of her wanderings and perhaps even suggesting an aborted attempt at escape.

Fig. 6. Making an escape?

WOMEN IN PERIL

Enveloped in the claustrophobic setting for days on end, Carol intentionally reinforces her isolation and, on the surface, such measures could be seen as familiar steps taken in horror cinema, usually to keep the exterior world and/or its dangers at bay (which is partly, to Carol's mind at least, the case here as well). But it is simultaneously encouraging the adverse entrapment from within. In this, *Repulsion* further correlates to films depicting heroines captured or confined and left to fight off invaders, Polanski's 'mini-genre' of what McKibbin calls 'inverted women in peril' (Orr/Ostrowska, 2006: 55). Aside from the director's own work in such a grouping (*Repulsion*, *Rosemary's Baby* and *Death and the Maiden* are McKibbin's examples), other non-Polanski films bearing similarities to *Repulsion* in this regard include Richard Loncraine's *The Haunting of Julia* (1977), which stars, like *Rosemary's Baby*, Mia Farrow. That film follows Farrow's frail and distraught Julia Lofting as she cuts herself off from her life and family, primarily her husband, driven by the desire to be alone and to come to terms with a disturbing psychological depletion. In her case, the desire stems from an apparent and clearly understandable incident: the death of her child, which she may have had a hand in when she attempted a frantic tracheotomy. Mary Henry (Candace Hilligoss) in Herk Harvey's *Carnival of Souls* (1962), like Julia, retreats as a reaction to a traumatic incident—a car accident—and in the wake of that opening disaster, she causes those around her to question her unfeeling disposition, with several of them stating she is 'cold,' that one can 'never know what she thinks' and that she is so quiet she 'fools you.' A priest cautions her against living in isolation, but as she flatly states, she doesn't desire the 'close company of other people' (all statements equally applicable to Carol's condition, were she and those around her more cognizant of her distress). There is also, in another film echoing several of *Repulsion*'s central themes, Brian De Palma's *Carrie* (1976), which features its titular female lead, played by Sissy Spacek, as vulnerable, sheltered and isolated, not by choice, but by the severe dictates of her oppressive mother (Piper Laurie). In De Palma's film, though Carrie is seen cowering in the shower, as in the first sequence (there with good reason), or later, when she retreats from her fellow students, she is not necessarily averse to being with others and wants to genuinely get along and go along. Like Carol, who seeks literal and symbolic shelter and resorts to violence when that haven is broached, there are also Thana (Zoë Lund), in Abel Ferrara's *Ms .45* (1981), who is already reserved as a result of her muteness and is tragically transformed by a series of rapes, and Camille Keaton's Jennifer in the 1978 version of *I Spit on Your Grave*, written and directed by Meir Zarchi, who seeks peaceful seclusion and is emotionally altered for the same brutal reason. And yet, *Repulsion* is something different. Unlike these other features, there is no clear reason for Carol's ailment, her social anxiety nor her consciously detrimental seclusion. What manipulates her behavior and her psychological bearing begins and ends (for as much as the film actually shows) within her own inner sphere of resolute reckoning. Even more than these other female victims, for Carol it is as Kier-La Janisse notes in her comprehensive *House of Psychotic Women*, a case where 'loneliness and alienation lead to a complex fantasy life that exists in dreams and hallucinations, facilitated by self-medication or sometimes just an imagination working overtime' (2016: 102).

Contrary to Carol in this way, Rosemary seeks and receives advice; she is aware of something not right and attempts to contextualize and rationalize these inexplicable episodes. She is anxious but also aware and vocal about her concerns, even if they are often ignored or downplayed; it's possible she is overthinking certain aspects of what is taking place, but the audience knows better. Though wracked with suspicion, Rosemary at least attempts to retain her independence, and when her nightmares become a little too real, she is, even in that position, mindful enough to know the difference, declaring during the film's satanic rape sequence, 'This is no dream. This is really happening!' Still, in that drugged, dream circumstance, she, like Carol, is nevertheless helpless. Corresponding to Rosemary, *The Tenant*'s Trelkovsky is a generally affable character as he enters his own chilling situation, which enables us to witness his gradual degeneration in a way not afforded with Carol, who is in the midst of the madness as the film commences and there is throughout the film little to no indication of how she functioned prior to this point. Opening with the intense close-up of Carol's eye, the first lingering shot of the film under its opening credits, we enter *Repulsion* as if in the middle of the story, as Bill Horrigan writes, 'but it's actually the beginning of the end' (2009). We are denied, in this narrative design, the true foundation of Carol's anxiety. While she appears to essentially create her horror out of the ordinary world, through her own conceptions and without any seeming control or assured consciousness of the ensuing development, someone like Trelkovsky is keenly aware of how his sense of normality is being subverted and thwarted, and it is accurate enough—to him and the viewer—that something isn't right, something that has nothing necessarily to do with his behavior; he remarks to a friend, for example, that there is 'Something odd going on in my building.' He is attentive to the plainly perceptible oddness, and having grown accustomed to his own daily habits and routines, the upending of normalcy is clear: 'At what precise moment,' he wonders aloud, 'does an individual stop becoming who he thinks he is?' Trelkovsky's aggressive neighbors *are* genuinely hostile; they are not, at least at first, pure figments of his imagination. He takes active measures to remove himself from the situation and although he displays a minorly anxious disposition, seen in his discomfort at church and in other social situations, Trelkovsky's relatively ordinary behavior intensifies as he declines into hysterics and paranoia, his delirium climaxing in actions that are suicidal not, like Carol, homicidal. Given *The Tenant*'s unsettling eccentricity, Polanski nonetheless argued against the comparison between it and *Repulsion*, at least on a tonal level, stating *The Tenant* is on a 'completely different register. *Repulsion* was not [meant to be] funny' (Greenberg, 2013: 138). Even so, writing on the *Sexual Violence and Female Experience in Roman Polanski's Apartment Trilogy*, Elise Moore observes, 'One way to describe *The Tenant* is to say that it starts out as *Rosemary's Baby*, with Trelkovsky's neighbors seemingly involved in a conspiracy against him that, however, may be his paranoid imaginings, and turns into *Repulsion*, with Trelkovsky revealed as a dangerous, delusional, and hallucinating madman whose beliefs can have only the most tenuous connection to reality' (2016).

Despite the perceived detachment between the viewer and Carol, due to her enigmatic manner, and between Carol and her own concept of a fixed reality, the engagement with her as a character remains strong, something largely attributable to Polanski's treatment of Deneuve and her first-rate performance. The twenty-one-year-old actress had recently risen to global stardom in Jacques Demy's *The Umbrellas of Cherbourg* (1964), and although Polanski auditioned a number of girls for the role of Carol (among them Francesca Annis, Compton's choice, whom Polanski would later cast as Lady Macbeth in his 1971 adaptation of Shakespeare's play), it would be Deneuve, a 'needless extravagance,' according to producer Klinger (Polanski, 1985: 200), who in *Repulsion* made her English-language debut. Years later, the Paris-born Deneuve would admit she was and remains scared of the dark, of empty, unfamiliar places, of silence and loneliness

Fig. 7. A Rorschach test of emotions.

(Criterion: 2009), genuine trepidations that must have surely added to her turn as the similarly afflicted Carol. And it is, with or without these real-life correlations, a tremendously sophisticated and triumphant performance based almost exclusively on physical articulation and, maybe more impressive, the deliberate withdrawal of such tell-tale expression. First seen holding an elderly customer's hand, the smoothness of Carol's spotless face contrasts with the crusty cake of beauty treatment applied to her patron, a graphic correlation initiated and repeated throughout the film as it emphasizes flesh, touch and Carol's staring at her own body in unaffected or conflated form, gazing at her reflection in a tea kettle, for example, distorted by the object to the point she has to turn her back to it. Her withdrawn posture, often hunched over, conveys the physically realized restriction of her emotional limitation, and although she becomes increasingly disheveled (her boss at one point comments on her unkempt hair), Carol is, in the words of Sam Adams, writing in the Los Angeles Times, 'both Rosemary and the devil in one unblemished package.' 'Even as she registers a growing sense of unease,' he writes, 'Deneuve retains the dislocated stare of a woman lost in a dream' (2009).

Repulsion was shot in coarse black and white by cinematographer Gilbert Taylor, who was at this point best known for his work with Stanley Kubrick, on 1964's *Dr. Strangelove or: How I Learned to Stop Worrying and Love the Bomb*, and Richard Lester, on his 1964 vehicle for The Beatles, *A Hard Day's Night*. Although his graphic contributions to *Repulsion* are undeniably effective, Taylor was perturbed by what Polanski was asking when it came to filming the radiant Deneuve in close-up with a disfiguring wide-angle lens: 'I hate doing this to a beautiful woman,' he lamented (Polanski, 1985: 204). Wearing almost no makeup, charted as the usually sole focus of Taylor's camera, Carol initially 'seems like the most Hitchcockian of blondes,' according to Michael Wojtas, 'impossibly remote and almost objectively beautiful. […] and her psychosexual collapse begins banally enough, welling up from the grotesque particulars of the everyday.' Yet, he continues, 'as Polanski's camera continually sticks close to Deneuve's perspective, Carol begins to function as a retort to the stereotype of the "icy blonde," a run of female archetypes Hitchcock purportedly created simply because they photographed well in black and white' (Wojtas). On this Hitchcock comparison, Moore additionally notes:

> *Repulsion*'s wonderful innovation is to combine Hitchcock's Norman Bates [the murderously multifaceted villain in 1960's *Psycho*] and *Marnie* (the eponymous heroine of the 1964 film) in a single protagonist, and in the process deconstruct a certain long-standing Western archetype of femininity whose most recent pop culture iteration, at the time, was the so-called "Hitchcock blonde." The coolness and remoteness of Hitchcock's blondes signify their ladylike refusal of carnality; and in this dichotomy, sexuality is male and sullying. In *Repulsion*, however, Deneuve's Carole is remote not because she's a lady, but because all of her interest in focused on an inner life that is absolutely inaccessible (2016)

Expressionless yet clearly terrified, mysterious and undefinable, Deneuve is a something of a Rorschach test of emotions, as one scrutinizes her behavior in an attempt to discern what she is feeling, to anticipate what she will do and to breach her otherwise inscrutable remoteness and diffidence. And still, as 'ultimately indefinable as she may be,' Wojtas contends, 'Carol is a unique, fully formed character rather than a mere tool for torturing the subconscious of brooding men, as are the important women in even the best of Hitch's films (*Vertigo, Rear Window*)' (Wojtas). She is strikingly beautiful, no doubt, but there is far more to her person than outward appearance. (As it happened, while Deneuve refused to appear nude in the film, she was asked by Polanski to pose for Playboy Magazine, a promotional gimmick she later regretted.) Her body is a recurring point of emphasis, for herself—biting her nails, her physical tics, washing her feet in the bathroom sink—and for what the camera sees—watching her undress into a transparent slip and revealing the slightest bit of upper leg, which also gets the attention of the randy landlord. For all that Deneuve and Polanski deny as far as getting inside Carol's riddled mind, obfuscating a full emersion in her psyche, what is clear, in any case, is that through the deft combination of Polanski's direction and Deneuve's appearance and performance, physicality and vulnerability are inexorably entwined, and they inevitably come to the fore when isolated and accentuated.

CHAPTER 2: SEX AND TERROR

Fig. 8. 'The nightmare world of a Virgin's dreams becomes the screen's shocking reality.'

Sold with the sensationalistic tagline, 'The nightmare world of a Virgin's dreams becomes the screen's shocking reality.' *Repulsion* situates Carol's sexual anxiety as a fundamental stimulus for the film's proceeding horror. And Polanski's corresponding sexualization of Deneuve is respectively twofold, as she is frequently seen at home in various stages of undress, yielding an enticing yet ingenuous impression (the physically exposed predisposition of a young woman being a recurrent horror device since nearly the dawn of the genre), while her public appearance is subject to lewd sidewalk catcalls and a series of unwanted advances. At her place of work, Carol overhears charges of masculine cruelty and coercion, a provocative admonition that likely generates the fear when she is herself confronted by aggressive male contact; the nascent violence kindled by a man's carnal belligerence meets her own primed response, engendered by the civic caution and magnified by her volatility. Plagued by sexual repression, Carol is further haunted by the sounds of her sister, Helen, in the breathy throes of passion with her boyfriend, Michael, whose disconcerting presence is manifest in lingering toiletries and a discarded undershirt. As a comprehensive corollary, Carol's alarming rape fantasies are countered by the essentially good-natured flirtations of Colin, as when a languid Carol is kissed by Colin and immediately, in a manic display of psychosexual revulsion, flees his embrace, nearly getting hit by a car in the process, rushing indoors, furiously wiping her lips and brushing her teeth in hysterical desperation. Throughout, in these and other instances, *Repulsion* conveys the consequent linkage of sex and horror through the embodiment of an attractive, susceptible female figure and her gendered experience.

THE MEN IN HER LIFE

It is little wonder a primary agent for Carol's revulsion is men, considering how the male sex is routinely presented and discussed in the film (perhaps, as it turns out, with some justification). Michael is indeed callous and inconsiderate, often with sex and little else on his mind (he is, after all, an adulterer, and is at one point seen unabashedly pinching Helen's behind), and Carol's appalled reaction to his leaving his toothbrush in her glass and the sexual sounds of his and Helen's lovemaking is not unreasonable. For an advancing example of how outside influences perpetually cloud her perspective of male-female affiliation, in some sense planting the seeds of her sexually-charged abhorrence, one need look no further than those who surround her at work: her older boss, a few younger coworkers and elderly patrons, one of whom is introduced in an abrasive close-up of her mouth as she fervently condemns men. These women, whether they know it or not, hold considerable sway over Carol, who is clearly amenable to their judgment. The beauty parlor where Carol works is, according to Moore, 'an all-female realm where solidarity is formed over the headaches doled out by "bitchy" bosses and clients and the heartaches occasioned by "filthy" men,' and those men, as Moore also points out, are contrastingly seen in the 'all-male realm of the pub frequented by Colin and his cronies, where bonding happens over filthy jokes and stories' (2016). The depiction of gender-based enmity has been a prime facet of Polanski's filmography, from his first feature, *Knife in the Water*, where its snare of two men and one woman is amplified by the strong current of sexual tension and animosity, to *Carnage*, arguably Polanski's most humorous film, which is fueled by the on-again, off-again pitting of the two men against the two women. And certainly, *Bitter Moon* takes sexual contention and competition as its vindictive central focus. Similarly, the world around Carol is one of preexisting frictions between the sexes, a contention that is essentially mild and normal, if not exactly healthy, but one which she observes and skews in accordance to what is already an unstable view of interpersonal interaction. It is also, crucially, a friction about sex and its timorous repression. *Repulsion* may be set in the era of London during the 'swinging' 1960s, but Carol is far removed from that atmosphere of sexual permissiveness. Accosted by a worker resting along the street, who beckons Carol with 'Hello darling, how about a bit of the other then?' she is also referred to by Colin's friends as 'Little Miss Muffet' ('Still keeping her legs crossed?') and is subjected to the landlord's sexual attempts at bribery, reaching some sort of 'arrangement' regarding his excusing of late rent payment. It is no wonder Carol is, as Elaine Macintyre states, 'passive and listless as the dead rabbit' and 'feels that women are nothing more than pieces of meat to be used and abused' (Macintyre).

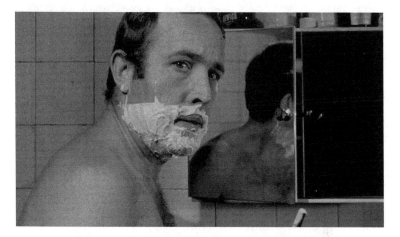

Fig. 9. An anodyne invasion is an invasion all the same.

To be sure, most of the men are crude, but the cast of their prospective endangerment is amplified by Carol's exceptional vulnerability, even when she herself isn't present in a scene (like at the pub, where even Colin grows annoyed by the incessantly coarse remarks of his cohorts, remarks that at times explicitly refer to Carol's sexual potential). Otherwise, she is generally kept at a distance in *Repulsion*, not only from the other characters but in terms of her on-screen presentation. Particularly in her relationships with, and her responses to, the various men in her life (so much as any of them are actually a part of her life), she is timid, unenthusiastic and disconnected. As an itemized extension of this, her aversion to the bathroom products and elements of clothing left behind by Michael are not just emblematic of an invasion of her safe space, but derive their connotative significance as indiscreet remnants of his masculinity and his physical body. Witnessing the shock of Michael simply shaving, itself an anodyne event, her reaction still evokes an outrageous and outraged terror. The razor, the toothbrush, his dirty undershirt: these otherwise innocuous fragments of Michael's daily routine become, in Carol's eyes, strangely sexual signifiers that are, at least at first, unwanted; while she thinks nothing of tossing his shirt in the trash, even as she hesitates to merely touch it, she nevertheless sniffs it then retches, and the constant displacement of the shirt—it will reappear in a hallway, later draped over the bed rail and she clings to it during one of the fantasy rape sequences—suggests an uncanny object with a certain magnetism she can't let go of, a perverse fascination. *Repulsion*, here and elsewhere, is 'all about sexual symbolism,' according to Kate Hagen, and the checklist of examples includes 'a tear in a bedside wall Carol can't stop fingering, a candlestick used as a blunt murder weapon, a platter of that persistently decaying rabbit with a man's straight razor in its blood, the rabbit's heart carried in Carol's handbag, potatoes that have sprouted, seeping bathroom walls.' While Hagen acknowledges the obviousness of such symbolism to today's viewers, as she correctly notes, 'to present such an imagistic look at a modern London woman's fear of sexuality and men in 1965 was truly radical' (2016). As representative imagery and in some cases catalysts for Carol's sexual anxiety, these same objects will resurface as items of explosive violence, linking, as much else in *Repulsion*, the volatile connection between sex and violence, desire and horror.

But among the male figures, the most complicated threat intimidating Carol, if he can even be considered a threat for most of the film, is Colin, who appears to truly care for the young woman and wants to establish a conventional heterosexual relationship with her. The mannered interactions between the two, as Adams alludes to in his L.A. Times article on the film, could be traced back to *Repulsion*'s screenplay, which 'had been contrived to require a minimum of dialogue, due to the relative unfamiliarity of both of its writers with the language in which it was to be filmed.' What dialogue there was, Adams notes, 'could as easily have been ad-libbed' and the 'fortuitous outcome of this was that conversations between Carol and Colin [...] which appear to be stilted onscreen (especially as many of them had to be post-synched over location footage) were considered to work to the film's advantage in terms of Carol's inability to relate to members of the opposite sex' (2009). It is only later in the picture, as Colin's frustrations mount—frustrations that may be born from sexual vexation as much as his struggle to forge any sort of conventionally personal rapport with Carol—that his behavior grows more inappropriate and overly aggressive, particularly in light of modern-day interpretations. One sees the conflicting perception of Colin's intentions in the choice of wording often used to describe his character and his actions. While critics have questioned whether or not Colin truly cares for Carol and wants to help, others, like Moore, note how he 'walks her, or *stalks her* to the doorway of her workplace' [italics added] (2016), while F.X. Feeney calls him Carol's 'tragic boyfriend' (2006: 106) and Peter Bradshaw, writing in The Guardian, states 'Carol is horrified by other men's desire for her, even when [Colin] is a transparently decent man whose honest love might be exactly what she needs' (2013). In any event, and whatever his intentions, the assessment of Colin is motivated most resoundingly by Carol's perception of his behavior. As is the case throughout *Repulsion*, the audience is reliant on her view of what is a hostile or at the very least an inappropriate, unwarranted and presumably unwanted gesture (even if it's often difficult to determine just what, exactly, Carol does want). And, proportionately, it's easy to see why such aggression frightens the poor girl. Discussing 'the ways in which the film reflects Carol's traumatic encounters with men,' Baker cites Jennifer M. Barker, who writes that *Repulsion* "'insidiously invites us to get close […] only to horrify us when those images begin to slither, creep, and erupt with things we'd rather keep at a distance.'" Thus 'exemplifying the alluring power of disgust as simultaneously fascinating yet frightening, the film's haptic texture, illuminated by Barker's use of "slither" and "creep," intensifies in parallel with Carol's disgust as she endures the touch of her assailants' (2018). When Colin barges into Carol's apartment it is, in fact, the first pure act of violent behavior that comes her way prior to the invasion of the landlord. His bursting through the door is a spontaneous, hostile action upsetting a confused, potentially hostile individual, so when Carol then attacks Colin with the candlestick holder, or later when she slashes wildly at the landlord with the razor, as Polanski places the camera 'in the POV of the suitor,' we feel, as Hagen observes, 'each desperate, trapped strike' (2016). The rape fantasies, so abstruse in terms of Carol's receptiveness, have come alive, and in real life, it is more than she can bear.

Fig. 10. The budding suitor arrives.

Carol cannot escape the overwhelming presence of male contact, and it is a contact habitually perceived as sinister and violent. For her, sex equals something like curious disgust if not death itself, and the initial phases of sexual interaction appear, to one as uninitiated as she, strange and intimidating. Still, despite Carol's reticence to engage in a literal sexual exchange, traces of her behavior suggest a latent, bewildered sexuality, creating an awkward and unfamiliar push-pull dynamic where eventual violence is the end result. The celibate depiction of Carol points to the 'stereotype of the chaste, virtuous female virgin,' as Harrington writes, 'who appears in horror films as both victim and hero [and] is defined explicitly in opposition to unbounded carnal female sexuality' (2018: 33). And it is this combination that arguably troubles Carol the most, as she tries to make sense of the disconcerting juxtaposition. Her sexual guilelessness is a veil that hides the brewing capacity for fierce response, and the amalgamation likewise drives much of *Repulsion* generally, as a film bearing significant elements of conjoined sex and violence (one of Colin's friends is intrigued by the prospect of a lover who also has a black belt in martial arts). Confronted by these numerous hazards, imagined or not, Carol defends herself in the only way she knows how, and her violent reactions are very much rooted in the enduring trials and tribulations of her gender and the seemingly boundless sexuality that surrounds her. It is finally with this ultimately fatal action by Colin that Carol releases an eruption of fury, and takes what, to her mind, is the only possible step. The torment has been steadily building to this point and is soon thereafter intensified with the attack of the landlord, whose behavior and impetus is plainly sexual in nature, whereas Colin's intentions, however poorly enacted, appear sincerely virtuous.

TRAUMA, VENGEANCE AND THE GAZE

Carol's violent response to the trauma that befalls her, coupled with and enhanced by her unstable mental condition, could thusly be compared to cinema's female vigilantes, who 'have a hard time distinguishing between people who want to hurt them and people in general' (Janisse, 2016: 71). Carol has, as we've seen, perpetual trouble making this distinction, which is why most everyone she encounters is perceived as intimidating or at least unpleasant. A young woman subjected to psychological scarring and abuse at home and in public would years later be the subject of *Carrie*, a film with numerous parallels to *Repulsion*, including sexual aversion, the gender-based confusion brought on by the norms and expectations of femininity and by the way her muddled emotions coalesce in a conclusion of violent retribution, which Carrie, to a certain extent in the beginning, performs as unwillingly as Carol. Concerning the connection between her sexuality and the aggressive acts, Shelley Stamp writes of the 'monstrous-feminine' in *Carrie*, where the girl's 'adolescent body becomes the site upon which monster and victim converge, and we are encouraged to postulate that a monster resides inside her' (Grant, 2000: 282). It's a more than seemly comparison to *Repulsion*, a film that likewise brings a young woman's sexuality front and center and then releases the related rage into an act of violence. Carrie's body is a prominent aspect of the film from its opening credits on, where the gushing blood of her first period causes her to fret over the apparent lack of control (or the lack of knowledge) of that very body. A woman (or women) who can't necessarily control her behavior is similarly prominent in another De Palma film, *Sisters*, from 1972, where its 'monstrous-feminine' takes shape in the supposed twin sisters Danielle and Dominique Blanchion (both played by Margot Kidder), the latter first appearing as a sexualized decoy for a television program called *Peeping Tom*. Minutes later, Danielle takes the male subject of the show back to her apartment where she is seen undressing as soon as she enters (much like Carol does when she is first seen at home in *Repulsion*) and, in a sequence not long after that, after the couple's lovemaking, she kills the visitor. Her aggression, as the film will eventually reveal, is also perhaps like Carol's in that it is based on the triggering of prior sexual anxieties. Similarly, Thana in *Ms. 45* is relentlessly subjected to crass men emerging from nearly every direction in her life, from the abrasive advances of her boss to the two men who rape her (sequences, like the fantasy rapes of *Repulsion*, shot in harrowing close-up), and the impact of sexualized gender-based initiation is further skewed in *I Spit on Your Grave*, when one of Jennifer's assailants, soon to be her victims, attempts to argue she instigated it with her sexuality.

Fig. 11. 'Victims of their bodies, victims of male attackers, and victims of a patriarchal society.'

Carol, not unlike the other women in these films, can't seem to win. Although she doesn't necessarily invite what occurs to her, whether it literally does or not (and the measure of her receptivity may, at times, be up for debate), when confronted with the ferocity to whatever degree, a violent lashing out seems the only concluding outcome, for lack of more familiar options. Though avoiding the violent retribution seen in *Repulsion* or *Carrie*, Carol's situation is equally paralleled in Polanski's own *Rosemary's*

Baby, for Carol and Rosemary are 'also at once the monsters and the victims of their films,' according to Moore, 'victims of their bodies, victims of male attackers, and victims of a patriarchal society.' It is, she notes, 'hardly unusual for the monster of a horror narrative to also be perceived as a victim,' but for Moore, who observes the intertwining of gender, subjectivity and horror in *Repulsion* and *Rosemary's Baby*, '*Repulsion* is an authentic representation of female sexual subjectivity because it highlights the madness-inducing contradictions in the social construction of femininity and female sexuality' (2016). Like Rosemary and Carrie, Carol's meekness and innocence is based to a considerable degree on her quintessence of femininity and associated gender expectancies.

Extending from the sexualization of Carol, which, while basically tasteful and realistic is nevertheless prominent in several instances of her appearance, scantily clad or nude with purposeful concealment, the importance of dress and appearance in the horror film—in most any horror film, particularly as it relates to female characters (for better or worse)—is something Italian horror maestro Dario Argento unashamedly alluded to when he stated, 'I like women, especially beautiful ones, if they have good face and figure, I would much prefer to watch them being murdered than an ugly girl or man' (Grant, 2000: 88). It's a troubling observation, certainly, and despite Argento's contention, Cwik argues that viewers 'don't want to see bad things happen to, or because of, a beautiful woman.' And yet, Cwik also notes, 'Polanski and Deneuve play off of the perverse desires of (straight male) viewers, who probably have more in common with the creeps doting on Carole [sic] than they're willing to admit' (2015). Of this rather overworked image of a female horror victim, however, Barry Keith Grant writes that typically, the vulnerability and sexuality are indeed heightened 'because she is a comely maiden "wearing [in the words of Harvey Roy Greenburg] a night-gown or a wedding-dress or some other light-coloured garment"' (2000: 5). (This recurring image is played for contrasting purposes in *Sisters*, with the color-coded attire of the apparent sisters; one, the good one, seen in white, the other, the ostensibly bad one, in black.) Because of this and other prominent aspects of filmic perception generally, critics like Carol J. Clover have noted how 'the cinematic gaze' is often said to be male, and just as the gaze '"knows" how to fetishize the female form in pornography [...] so it "knows," in horror, how to track a woman ascending a staircase in a scary house and how to study her face from an angle above as she first hears the killer's footfall' (Grant, 2000: 96). Polanski's own lingering on Carol isn't strictly sexual in nature, but it does revel in her physical frailty and exposure, making the impending terror, where through her imaginings she is variously assaulted, all the more glaring. One reason, Moore argues, that 'we feel that we are sharing the experiences of Carole [sic] and Rosemary is that we observe them in such intimate situations: we follow the half-nude (and sometimes completely nude) Carole around her apartment for days on end; we follow the anxieties and tribulations and terrors of Rosemary's pregnancy; we even closely observe them as they are being sexually assaulted.' Moore then questions the relationship between the viewer, via Polanski's camera, and the subject (Carol) itself, challenging Davide Caputo's notion that 'the observer, in the position of the tethered camera, is a "voyeur."' True, we are granted intimate access to Carol but there isn't anything necessarily surreptitious or intrusive about Polanski's camera choice or the actions seen. Writes Moore:

> The intimacy of what we witness; our access to the protagonists' purely subjective experiences; in *Repulsion*, the communication of the protagonist's state of mind by making us share her nausea; the fact that we are claustrophobically confined to characters who are claustrophobically confined: all of these things serve to bring us a great deal closer to the characters than the term "voyeur" suggests. We are indeed voyeurs, however, if that means being privy to intimate experiences that no one would normally observe and that, in the case of subjective mental experience, no one could observe (2016).

In her 1993 study, *The Monstrous-Feminine: Film, Feminism, Psychoanalysis*, Creed thoroughly explores many of these same concerns, remarking, for example, that 'the definition of sin/abjection as something which comes from *within* opens up the way to position woman as deceptively treacherous. She may appear pure and beautiful on the outside but evil may, nevertheless, reside within in. It is this stereotype of feminine evil— beautiful on the outside/corrupt within—that is so popular with patriarchal discourses about woman's evil nature' (2007: 42). Citing Gérard Lenne's article, *Monster and Victim: Women in the Horror Film*, Creed notes that he 'allows that there are female monsters but then finds reason why they are not real monsters; for instance he states that the female vampire exists but her role is usually "secondary"; the schizophrenic female monsters of *Repulsion* and *Sisters* are understandable because "schizophrenia is readily assimilated to female behavior'" (2007: 3-4). And recalling another horror staple, William Friedkin's *The Exorcist* (1973), where its sexual content is similarly embedded in its surface horror scenario, Creed submits that the connections 'drawn in the film between feminine desire, sexuality and abjection suggest that more is at stake than a simple case of demonic possession. Possession becomes the excuse for legitimizing a display of aberrant feminine behavior which is depicted as depraved, monstrous, abject–and perversely appealing' (2007: 31).

Akin to the vigilante, a character like Carol also parallels horror's so-called 'final girl,' in that she is, in the words of Clover, 'abject terror personified' (Grant, 2000: 82). 'Angry displays of force may belong to the male,' she writes, 'but crying, cowering, screaming, fainting, trembling, begging for mercy belong to the female. Abject terror, in short, is gendered feminine, and the more concerned a given film with that condition—and it is the essence of modern horror—the more likely the femaleness of the victim' (Grant, 2000: 96). Carol isn't quite completely this, however, at least in terms of her expressiveness in the face of terror. In truth, aside from the fleeting fear she shows when perceiving the apartment in its varying states of disruption or during the fantasy rape sequences, she rarely seems to register much emotion at all. All the same, this lack of response is partly why it is so unnerving, for there is no strong emotion to latch onto, no demonstrative outlet for the viewer to identify the fears. How, then, to make sense of her various responses, when her motivations are unclear and progressively ambiguous? As Hagen writes, 'It's one thing to present a female character who is a stark-raving lunatic and monstrous to those around her, but it's a much more impressive trick to create a protagonist like Carol, who is her own antagonist throughout the film' (2016). Even the rape sequences are far from obvious in terms of her engagement with the imaginary assailant (Moore notes how Carol puts on makeup 'in anticipation of her nightly visit […] which she does not seem to be in control of despite the fact that it's her fantasy, but when he attacks her, she remains terrified and struggles' [2016]). Suggesting the complexity of Carol's response to these rapes, there is thus the anticipation of it and the 'moment when it becomes a reality,' which is something, Moore notes, quite different, in that Carol's 'feelings about sex are violent, and apt to change from one violent extreme to the other, and to change depending on whether it's a distant object of contemplation or an immediate object of sensation. It doesn't seem to be possible for Carole, at this point, to feel anything but a violent reaction against sex when it's happening (or as close as she allows herself to get), which doesn't mean that these are her "real" feelings about it: they are all her real feelings about it' (2016).

RAPE AND THE POLANSKI DILEMMA

Concerning the male characters, particularly those who do end up as victims in *Repulsion*, Meikle states that although the film originates from 'a self-declared chauvinist,' despite this, '*Repulsion* is remarkably unsympathetic in its depiction of the males in the film: be they landlords, lovers or mere boyfriends, all of them lie' (2006: 79). Such comments inevitably lead to Polanski's treatment of Carol and other female characters throughout his career, characters who are often in peril and are frequently sexualized to a certain degree. And yet, there is considerable sympathy and understanding. Writing expansively on this very topic, Kim Morgan points to remarks made by film scholar Molly Haskell, author of the acclaimed and influential 1974 text *From Reverence to Rape: The Treatment of Women in the Movies*. Haskell, Morgan states, refers to the 'image of the anesthetized woman' in Polanski's work, 'the beautiful, inarticulate, and possibly even murderous somnambulate,' a point she generally concurs with. But she takes issues with the 'tired criticism that in all of Polanski's films, including *Repulsion*, "the titillations of torture are stronger than the bonds of empathy."' Rather, Morgan contends:

> Polanski's removed morality is exactly why he is often brilliant: He is so empathetic to his characters that, like a trauma victim floating above the pain, he is personally impersonal. He insightfully scrutinizes what is so frightening about being human, yet he doesn't feel the need to be resolute or sentimental about his cognizance. He is also, consciously or subconsciously, aware of the darkness he explores, especially in his female characters, who could be seen as extensions of himself (2017).

'Nerve-racking [and] so physically flawless that she often seems half human,' Morgan writes on the juxtaposing characteristics of Deneuve's Carol, calling her an 'anemic girl' and noting 'she can barely lift up her arm, yet at the same time she is highly sensual, an ample, heavily breathing woman with more than a glint of carnality in her dreamily vacant eyes.' Crucially, Morgan also observes the infantile nature of Carol (she is at one point in the film referred to as just that), stating that 'Deneuve makes one feel the confusion of a corrupted child: She is an arrested adolescent who, like an anorexic, cannot face her womanliness without visions of perverse opulence and violence' (2017). Instances are seen in Carol's occasionally juvenile manner (clinging to a stuffed dog), her meekness, her diminutive and delicate temperament and her dependency, especially on her sister's mere attendance, for the elder sibling is clearly the adult in this familial relationship. This is a similar character trait shared with Rosemary in *Rosemary's Baby*, a film that is quite reasonably rife with images and sounds relating to children, from its lyrical 'la-la-la' opening score to Rosemary's comparable state of prenatal dependence and vulnerability. 'Like Carol,' Leaming notes, 'Rosemary is childish, immature. Her outfits and manner suggest a little girl. Once she even calls her husband "Daddy"' (1981: 89).

Fig. 12. The 'personification of sexual mystery.'

Carol is, for Morgan, the 'personification of sexual mystery—she is what lurks beneath the orgasms of pleasure and pain,' and what Polanski finds intriguing, she writes, and revolting, is 'perceptively female, making *Repulsion* a woman's picture more than women may want to know, or care to face' (2017). Polanski himself noted in a 1990 interview with Gerhard Midding that *Repulsion* speaks to women in a perhaps surprising way. 'It was much more popular than I expected when it was released,' he said, 'something due mainly to female audiences' (Cronin, 2005: 140). As surprised as Polanski may have been at the time, his subsequent career has yielded more than its fair share of multifaceted female characters, many of whom are, like Carol, defined by the moral and social complexities identified with their sex. There is, for instance, *What?* (1972), where the sexuality of Sydne Rome's Nancy is conspicuous in much of the film, a film that likewise includes typical Polanski touches such as voyeurism and the frequent burden of repellent men. Nancy is a stranger in perhaps the strangest of Polanski's lands and is subject to the bizarre inner workings of an anteceding arena where her physicality puts her in something close to jeopardy, where sex and violence mingle with a certain bizarre hostility. *Chinatown*, too, progresses with the discovery that Evelyn Mulwray's (Dunaway) current predicament and troubled past is largely the result of psycho-sexual damage and paternal abuse; she is dismissed as a 'disturbed woman,' according to her vicious father, Noah Cross (John Huston). Then there is Tess, another young girl repeatedly at the mercy of men, her innocence and naivete tested and her physical features frequently the focus of these men as well as Polanski's camera. Ironically and hypocritically living under the stigma of her sexual experience, many of the male figures in this feature look on Tess as a sexual object above all else, and yet for her supposed transgressions she is constantly chided (one wonders how Carol would be perceived were she to similarly act on every sexual impulse that came her way). *Bitter Moon* contains a more overt use of sexuality as a tool in and of itself, where married couple Nigel and Fiona (Hugh Grant and Kristin Scott Thomas) are continually warned of Mimi's (Emmanuelle Seigner) sexual prowess and the potentially debilitating violence aligned with it: 'Beware of her,' cautions Peter Coyote's Oscar. 'She's a walking mantrap.' Mimi is a captivating, puzzling beauty full of mystery and malevolence, embodying the classic Polanski interplay of sex and violence bound in black overcoat, at one point brandishing a glistening razor and regularly conveying a perverse fascination with disturbing, sadistic torment. Take as well the aforementioned vulnerability of Paulina Escobar in *Death and the Maiden*, who stuffs her panties into the mouth of Dr. Miranda, something of a reversal of the prior sexual trauma that has riddled her past due to his earlier transgression. Also, like *Repulsion*, *Cul-de-sac* offers 'an odd view of women, either sexually repressed and mad or nymphomaniacal and castrative' (Leaming, 1981: 69), while *Rosemary's Baby* posits Rosemary's sex and her gender as a more specific compound for violence, and its sexual assault expresses a more conventionally monstrous rendering.

In a Roman Polanski film that does have such a strong central focus on a female character, there emerges in *Repulsion*, certainly in retrospect, undeniable complications in terms of Polanski himself. On one hand, there is the history of Polanski's relationship with his actresses, which has at times been quite contentious (trouble with Jolanta Umecka on the set of *Knife in the Water*, a combative relationship with Yvonne Furneaux while making *Repulsion*, unkindly provoking Faye Dunaway during the making of *Chinatown*). Additionally, and this ventures into more precarious territory, there is the way Polanski's treatment of Carol inescapably calls to mind his subsequent history, as relevant as much as it is a distraction given *Repulsion* came out more than a decade before the incident that would forever alter Polanski's life and career. This incident, of course, is the 1977 conviction of his drugging and raping a 13-year-old girl, a case endemic with alarming details, intricate legal maneuverings and a persistent range of controversial commentary. As summarized by James Greenberg, Polanski 'agreed to a plea bargain in which he admitted having unlawful sexual intercourse with a minor, fulfilled about half of a ninety-day court order for psychiatric evaluation and expected to be released on probation' (2013: 11). At that point, as Polanski tells it, 'the judge then reneged on the bargain-plea that was accepted by all sides' (Cronin, 2005: 191), and with additional, indeterminate prison time possible, Polanski left for Europe and has not returned to the United States since. *Repulsion* was released well before this time, though, and it is hardly the only Polanski film to feature the vexing yet sympathetic treatment of a female lead.

Nevertheless, the film's sensitivity to the female experience, in its 'own skewed way,' is noteworthy even before one considers, as Moore does, 'that the auteur helming the film is now equally well known as both a master of suffocating misé-en-scene and a fugitive rapist' (2016). Considering just this, though, especially with regards to *Repulsion*, she reckons with the problematic nature of Polanski the perceptive filmmaker and the convicted criminal: 'How could an artist perform the exceptional act of empathy that is cross-gender identification, yet commit the profound failure of basic empathy that is how we normally conceive of rape? What does that say about art, empathy, and rape?' As she watched Polanski's films with this question in the back of her mind, Moore states, she 'registered the prevalence of rape as a subject in his films, and it became impossible to believe that the theme of *Repulsion* was just a coincidence and that Polanski, in the guise of a hedonistic, chauvinistic 1970s Hollywood director, committed rape despite his ability to empathize, as an artist, with victims of that kind of assault.' For her, it is 'more than a movie,' 'but, as the movie it is, it's also more than a painful emblem of the horror of being female. While certainly capturing the trauma of sexual abuse, Polanski did not make a grim, realistic study of PTSD, but rather (perhaps plucking his tone from Hitchcock's *Psycho*) a sly black comedy that, among other things, deconstructs the cultural ideal represented by his blonde child-woman heroine' (2016). Likewise, Jenna Ipcar sees the irony in the fact a convicted rapist 'could have ever written and directed such an intensely empathetic and socially enlightened film [...] a movie that focuses on how societal pressures around sex and gender drive one woman to madness, murder, and then a catatonic state' (2018).

There is little to add to the insightful, considerate comments of these female critics, and, in any case, the rape delusions/fantasies are irrefutably prominent throughout *Repulsion*, and taken solely in the context of the film itself, they are not without considerable narrative, thematic and visual complexity. 'The manner in which *Repulsion* portrays the violation of Carole [sic] slightly *reduces* the horror of the rape as it is anchored in a hallucinatory content,' argues Caputo, who details the aesthetic of these sequences as both a way to experience Carol's terror and as a semi-distancing technique on Polanski's behalf (perhaps itself evoking Carol's own psychological detachment). 'The horror is instead mostly derived from witnessing the character to whom we are tethered experience such horrific hallucinations due to her increasingly tenuous grasp of reality. As disturbing as the rape scenes are [...] we remain quite certain that the events *are not really happening*' (2012: 126). Real or not, rape as an act of horror and as a common element in films beyond the straightforward horror genre, does have considerable consequence, not all of which is necessarily negative. As Moore acknowledges, principally in terms of Polanski's formal depiction of Carol's assorted rapes:

> There are many advantages to using a surrealistic dream sequence to depict a rape. First, to objectively show a woman being raped by a monster while surrounded by elderly naked witches would not only give away the game but be at once unbearable to watch and so ridiculous that the audience could not emotionally accept the reality of the horror. On the other hand, to realistically depict a rape from the victim's point of view would be so harrowing as to test the limits of representation (2016).

Janisse, for her part, sees the positive in such a traumatic event, at least as far as what it opens up in a film's storyline. 'Female audiences often complain about the presence of rape scenes in films,' she writes, 'These scenes are cited as exploitative and their directors labelled misogynists. But they don't realize that rape scene is the single greatest justification for anything else in the film that follows – no matter how illogical, unbelievable, sadistic, misanthropic, graphic or tortuous. The audience will accept any direction the story takes because culturally, rape is worse than death.' 'While many manifestations of neurosis are triggered by external factors,' she adds, 'rape is especially tragic in that it always results in neurosis' (2016: 50).

Unlike cases in the rape-revenge subgenre, however, where, as Harrington advises, citing Martin Fradley, "'Rape and sexual objectification serve […] as a catalyst for an expressionistic violence which offers a way of talking about the violent (re-)emergence of a feminist political consciousness" (2018: 73-74), what happens to Carol in *Repulsion* seems to occur, per Laine, 'without any narrative motivation,' the effects of which 'is the devastating, schizophrenic terror of being unable to trust one's own senses. But again, it is the film itself that forces the spectators to live through this effect rather than to merely imagine it' (2011). Less ambiguous is the clear centrality of Carol's gender, and the way, notes Baker, who refers to the way she applies the lipstick and irons Michael's undershirt (with the iron unplugged), 'Carol's violent fantasies can, to an extent, be understood as a consequence of her unsuccessful refusal to form a gendered cultural identity.' For Baker, Polanski exemplifies trauma as 'central to the construction of the woman, suggesting that even if Carol were to adhere to the domestic feminine ideal, she would nonetheless succumb to male domination.' In this vein, she notes, 'the spectator may feel uncomfortable also in extra-cinematic ways today when watching the spectacle of sexual violence enacted against women presented as androgynously innocent and young, despite the fact that *Repulsion* contains a spectacle of revenge at its close, however ambivalent we might feel about its incorporation into a patriarchal genre and setting' (2018). Compounding these issues is the corresponding nature of Polanski's 'monstrous,' whether it is quite literally growing inside Rosemary (Helena Goscilo refers to the 'bodily invasion' of both *Rosemary's Baby* and *Repulsion* [Orr/Ostrowska, 2006: 29), or, as it is with Carol, when she becomes something of her own worst enemy, both cases rousing the question of what role these films play with regards to what Le Cain calls the 'horror staple of the vulnerable female in jeopardy.' In *Repulsion*, he writes, 'the icily beautiful Carol is disturbing in her vacancy, her lack of character, her unformed-ness as a person, veering between insecure timidity and murderous self-defence that never grows into self-assertion' (Orr/Ostrowska, 2006: 123). In both *Repulsion* and *Rosemary's Baby*, 'gendered experience engenders horror,' and for Moore, the horror 'has to do with living in a female body, due both to physical facts about such bodies and to the social construction of gender.' But in contrast to *Rosemary's Baby*, where the horror is 'always in what is happening to Rosemary,' Carol's 'mental theatre' is an 'additional source of horror, as her mind gives way under the stress of her gendered experience.' In both films, Moore concludes, 'because the heroines' experience is where most of the horror in the films is located, the viewer is made to share that experience, even as we retain enough distance from Carole and Rosemary to be horrified by, as well as with, Carole, and to doubt Rosemary's judgment' (2016).

Carol is clearly exposed in a vulnerable way, through her clothing and personality and performance, but once her disturbed mind is given a violent, physical realization, the identification shifts as she becomes a danger, not just to herself, which was assumed from the start, but to others. 'By positioning women in the role of victim, killer or warrior,' writes Caputo, 'a greater emotional response is elicited from the audiences due to what stereotypes inform us is the female gender's "inherent" vulnerability' (2012: 174). So, while there is some justification concerning why Carol positions those on the receiving end of her wrath (especially the landlord), there is also the concern that others close to her or even remotely kind may similarly suffer the consequences of their association. But even that would not be without understanding. The terror Carol feels is pervasive, as unavoidable as her own body, which is perhaps why, in moments of dazed delirium or panic, her physical features are so often the focus of what she and the spectator views. For Carol, the apparent preoccupation with her own self is countered by the revulsion she expresses when it comes to the body of others, particularly Michael's, and, by extension, the items she associates with his physical presence. It's an opposing perception weighed against the more familiar instances where female bodily functions 'have long been patriarchally figured as abject.' *Repulsion*, Baker points out:

> enacts a reversal of this virile practice, in which it is the belongings of men that are
> dispelled and rendered disgusting by Carol. Invoking a Kristevan notion of abjection,

Carol's disgust with items that have been exposed to Michael's skin and saliva exemplifies both the corrupting nature of the male sex as threatening her mental order and the film's preoccupation with disgusting bodies. This male defilement, which only intensifies as Carol's psychosis worsens and imaginary men break into her home, again reflects the pervasive nature of trauma (2018).

This border between male and female is likewise evoked and twisted in *The Tenant*, where Trelkovsky takes to becoming the former tenant of his current apartment, a deceased female, and the unease caused by him 'is not that his masquerade produces confusion, but that it calls attention to, and juxtaposes, differences.' Given that Trelkovsky 'makes such an unsuccessful man,' notes Moore, 'mild-mannered and tiny-statured, it seems strikingly unfair that he should be too masculine to make a successful woman, but Polanski makes no attempt to ameliorate the details, the hairy arms and bulky calves, that show us the gap between Trelkovsky's fantasy and reality. And it is this gap, as in the scene where Carole gives herself a clown-mouth in preparation for her unavoidable "date," like a child who doesn't know how to use makeup, that makes him grotesque: what Diane Arbus called "the gap between intention and effect"' (2016).

Though referring to teen horror movies (not exactly *Repulsion* territory but fitting nonetheless), Martin Fradley asserts that such films 'deal with "young women's everyday gendered discontent," and recycle and rearticulate a key trope in postfeminist cinema: "women who embrace violence as a refusal of victimhood"' (Harrington, 2018: 73). See *Carrie*, for example, a decent girl who is tormented to no end by most of those around her. The exceptional cruelty she faces is owed to her adolescent situation and that of others, while Carol's is a more adult torment, largely sexual in nature but suggesting the same sort of innocence. And just as 'few critics fail to see Carrie as a monster in some sense, [viewing] the havoc she wrecks as a positive rebellion against oppression' (Shelly Stamp Lindsey, quoted in Grant: 281), there is a similar sense of acting out in a vindicated fashion in *Repulsion*, and one is tempted to rally behind Carol's cause, relating to the oppression and sympathizing despite the horror depicted. Of course, this can also be viewed in a contradictory fashion, due in part to Carol's psychotic condition. 'Unlike her comparatively-lauded male counterpart—"the eccentric,"' writes Janisse, 'the female neurotic lives a shamed existence. But the shame itself is a trap—one that is fiercely protected by men and women alike' (2016: 8).

CHAPTER 3: PARANOIA AND PERCEPTION

Fig. 13. Entering the mind of madness.

As a possible outgrowth of his youthful persecution, Polanski populates his films with characters gripped by a manifold, variously realized sense of paranoia. Whereas Rosemary's suspicion in *Rosemary's Baby* appears well-founded and she earnestly attempts to convey her distress, and unlike the 'everyone's-out-to-get-me' conspiracies of *Frantic*, *The Ninth Gate*, and *The Ghost Writer*—effectively unsettling because they're true—Carol's schizophrenia in *Repulsion* is traumatically isolated and internalized. Although her psychological concerns are discernable at home and in certain social situations, contributing to the film's presentation of overwhelming, unbounded fear, the notion of what is or isn't actually happening suits a complementary horror convention which permits the anomalous as ostensibly plausible if it derives from an unsound mind. Accordingly, starting with the eye that opens *Repulsion*, 'considered to be the mother of all "neurotic women" horror movies' (Janisse, 2016: 57), Polanski signals the film's preoccupation with subjective and sensitive (and sometimes squirm-inducing) perception. He adopts, and the film therefore accepts, the viewpoint of Carol's troubled contemplation (as necessitated by an engrossing narrative), manipulating the spectator's own unsettled view in the process. As Carol surveys the ruffled sheets where Helen and Michael slept, or when she fixates on cracks in the sidewalk, one must decipher the significance of the presumed menace, for much of *Repulsion*'s horror is derived from a semi-stunted engagement with Carol as a sympathetic protagonist. For Carol, though, the terror is real, and the features that have no apparent consequence in and of themselves prove vital because they so affect her well-being. Carol's inner rigidity finds an outlet in Deneuve's unnerving physical performance: chewing on her hair, constantly brushing away something that isn't there, her shifting wide eyes and open mouth etching an implicit fear upon an otherwise placid face. A recoiling Carol, meanwhile, appears ready to pounce and hide at the same time, highlighting the latent ferocity, while escalating audio-visual eruptions and her reciprocal response, or lack thereof, are means by which to gauge her emotional withdrawal. On the one hand, Carol's handling of a glistening straight razor and the immediate cut to her sister using a knife to peel potatoes links the increasing prevalence of potential danger, just as a throwaway line about the minister of health discovering eels in his sink suggests a portentous, off-kilter world. On the other, *Repulsion*'s emphasis on inexplicable action (Carol scrawling an invisible something on a window, perhaps a vain attempt to communicate) works to develop the unease of abnormal behavior presented and enacted as typical and persistent.

THE PARANOID PERSPECTIVE

Again, this is a common thread uniting the films of Polanski's Apartment Trilogy, with *The Tenant* in particular being a study of paranoia, according to Meikle, 'without peer,' a 'languid and closely-observed muse on alienation and mental disintegration [...] the culmination of where [Polanski] and Brach began in *Repulsion*' (2016: 89). Similarly, Caputo sees the same horror present in both *The Tenant* and *Rosemary's Baby*, 'where it is not so much the spectre of the supernatural that terrifies (which remains, in any case, unresolved in both films), but rather the character's inability to "grasp" the world,' an horrific failure augmented by the enigmatic endings, 'which serve to similarly upset the spectators own ability to "grasp" a stable diegetic reality' (2012: 112). Following the characters of these three films, and the unexplained phenomena that grips them and never lets them off the hook, Polanski creates a lingering uncertainty and the horror of something unresolved and unexplained. And in all three cases, there is no satisfying horror movie rescue or sense of salvation. But by locating the viewer in the mind's eye of Carol, Polanski induces a persuasive degree of empathy even if a complete discernment is lacking, so that, as Moore writes, 'We understand that Carole is paranoid from her actions, and we understand that Rosemary is paranoid from her words, but there is no attempt to visually represent a "paranoid perspective" on the other characters.' The one partial exception in *Repulsion*, she notes, is the camera's attention to the workman after Carol passes him:

> The shot conveys Carole's sexual paranoia to the viewer and makes us share it by briefly giving it seeming objective confirmation; however, even here, the man's expression is arguably not intrinsically sinister, but is made so by the way in which it is shot: the expressive camera movement, with the camera, up until then following Carole, suddenly gravitating toward him (like Carole's attention, or anxiety); the way his face seems to veer dangerously close to the viewer as the camera passes him; and the way the bright light and stark shadows emphasize the crack-like lines on his face and spaces between his teeth, inducing us, as with the shots of the elderly women's faces in the beauty parlor, to contemplate the nausea-inducing, inhuman qualities of the human face. We are not, that is, given a version of the man that only Carole sees, which would serve to underline the discontinuity between her perception and reality; rather, the camera, standing in for Carole's paranoid frame of mind, shows us how she can see him this way, which underlines the continuity between her perception and reality (2016).

By contrast, there is *Rosemary's Baby*, where, as Greenburg remarks, 'What made the story shocking was that Rosemary was a vulnerable girl from Omaha living an everyday life in the big city that little by little goes haywire. In the context of the film, it was something that could happen to any unsuspecting soul' (2013: 83). Carol is at more of a remove than this, though, for we are never afforded the time to relate to her and see her prior to her descent. There are, however, slight allusions made to what might be a persistent, preexisting issue with Carol. She asks Helen if she is still going away, to which her sister replies, 'Don't start that again' (her concern has evidently been voiced before, at least once), while Carol's boss observes that she is *still* biting her nails. Carol has, even if perhaps only in gestating stages, apparently been behaving like this for some time, for

what has been seen and voiced in the short duration of the film to this point hardly seems like enough to elicit such an exasperated reaction from those perturbed by her behavior. There is a sense of unreality from the start either way, with Carol's lost, dreamy gaze commented upon in the film's first scene (three times in all do those around Carol ask if she is asleep or comment that she must be dreaming); her pensive innocence clearly belies something deeper, something more profound, feelings compounded by her catatonic wanderings, the discordant drums and cymbals crashing on the soundtrack and the shifting perception of her neuroses, the staggered impression of her anxiety. This impression is willfully skewed, in the tea kettle for example, where she is inducing the skewing, anticipating it, wanting it, while other times it is cinematically contrived to depict her mental distortion with visual variation.

While *Repulsion* gave way to the all-encompassing paranoia and cultish plot of *Rosemary's Baby*, where the horror 'lies not in Rosemary's paranoid imagining of ills that are not there but in her inability to imagine the evils everywhere around her, however instantly visible they are' (Morrison, 2007: 61), the opposite appears the case with Carol's brand of paranoia, where every surrounding feature of her existence bears a potential threat. Rosemary refuses, at least at first, to confront what seems so obviously amiss, yet as her dreams torment her, 'with the half-knowledge that she cannot escape into herself,' that dream space becomes 'horribly permeable, letting demons out and monsters in [...] further evidence of the dissolution of a boundary that, even if it was never really there, might have preserved an order in which things could be just what they were and people could dream in peace' (Morrison, 2007: 73). With the carryover of her supposed dream state into a very real actuality, Rosemary lacks, like Carol, any escape from what hounds her, and moving toward *The Tenant* as the cycle continues, 'the fears explored grow more abstract.' As Wojtas writes, in that film, 'Polanski, playing his own protagonist, is in danger of losing his barely-there personality as he seemingly absorbs the spiritual imprint of the suicidal woman who previously lived in his apartment' (Wojtas). Again, though, Polanski provides a glimpse of him prior to the madness and we see the obvious external factors that contribute to his delirium. It's no more rational, perhaps, but the context presents the descent in more relatable, step-by-step fashion, with a certain amount of understanding and comprehension and a different sort of sympathy.

Fig. 14. Seeking out the distortion.

For all of her aversion, less like Rosemary but somewhat like Trelkovsky in this respect, Carol almost seems to seek out these points of revulsion in a form of masochistic torture, testing herself, prompting the hallucinations and the nightmares, unable to fully remove herself from the horror as a result. She is drawn to the abject as it, in the words of Peter Hutchings, 'offers a source of fascination and desire' (2004: 36), which is much the same for the viewer and is a response integral to the horror film generally, particularly with regard to its relatively modern trappings of explicit or at least exceptional gore and other unsettling features that can't help but draw our attention, which is partly the point of the genre's fantastic acceptance. These features, however, are largely absent in *Repulsion*, for it is a film deriving its terror from a progressive, subtly escalating menace. 'For all its shock tactics, *Repulsion* is remarkably cold-blooded,' notes Adams. 'You have the feeling you're being manipulated by a master, one whose hands never sweat and whose eye never blinks' (2009). To that end, as Polanski controls the environment of *Repulsion*, he does so with a knowing sense of what is or isn't working in terms of the film's percolating trepidation, recognizing that not everything has significance and will carry later importance, but the fact that anything might is part of the film's central terror, for we are never certain how Carol will integrate any given object into her agitation (she sees a crack in the sidewalk before she ever sees or comments on similar fissures within the house itself, perchance signaling the way in which she consumes outside influences). As with *Rosemary's Baby*, *The Tenant* and *The Ninth Gate*, Orr notes that the imagining of the worse can lead to insanity, unlike *Chinatown* and *The Pianist*, where 'actual experience of the worst leads to a different impulse, that is to retain one's sanity and cling onto life at all costs' (Orr/ Ostrowska, 2006: 19), so as we/Carol witness signs of something seemingly abnormal or theoretically striking, like cracks in the sidewalk, which literally stop Carol in her tracks, the objects in and of themselves, however innocuous they may seem, become outstanding via Polanski's camera as it similarly picks up from Carol's own attentive focus. This fundamental process is 'characteristic of, and necessary to, the modern horror film,' according to Schneider, where its overriding terror is 'neither its monster nor its typical narrative patterns, but rather a specific spectatorial affect, namely anxiety' (2009: 25). It is during these moments, 'when it is simply impossible to discern, long into the narrative, whether or not things are what they seem' that 'everything on screen, all interiors, exteriors, characters, and their interactions, are imbued with dread import' (Schneider, 2009: 145).

Fig. 15. The eye opens.

With the opening close-up of an eye, pulling back to disclose the bewildered face that surrounds the eye, belonging to a zombified Carol, united by a slow drum beat over the opening credits of *Repulsion* (the slicing scrawl of the titles designed by Maurice

Binder), Polanski puts us immediately and uncomfortably close to Carol's subjectivity, and like much else in the film, the image is held for a longer than normal duration; the uncertainty and the pounding refrain of the music prove ominous and unnerving. From there, Polanski's 'eloquent, persuasive translation of psychological disintegration into physical/physiological terms' (Orr/Ostrowska, 2006: 30), and the rendering of Carol's psyche and the related manipulations of her physical being, take shape in Deneuve's underrated performance, which is somewhat unique in the horror film, certainly of the period, where so much is dependent on one person to carry the feature and to express what he or she can't so otherwise, due to their inarticulateness or their the nature of their placement within the narrative, as a solitary individual who has little interaction or, at most, a disjointed interaction, with others through whom he/she can express their fears. 'There can't be,' as Peter Bradshaw argues, 'many other films which so plausibly show an entire, warped world created from a single point of view' (2013), and to this end, as Cwik also points out, 'Polanski delves deeper into the ruinous mind of a damaged, desecrated woman than any other director had done before, excavating the contradictions and afflictions of her undefined "problem" and erecting a nightmarish world that reflects her point of view' (2015). Moving in a way that is both wooden and fitful, Carol appears uncomfortable in any situation, rubbing her nose, shuffling her body, looking at herself in much the same inquisitive way as we do, perhaps recognizing the monster looking back, the monster within, the monster that appears, in this case, in what is surely an uncommon form. As a schizophrenic personality, Carol represents the disorder as Ewa Mazierska describes, as one who 'remains at a distance from his own perceptions and thoughts, to the point of failing to recognize himself, his physical body, as belonging to him' (2007: 37). This is conceivably why Carol so willingly gives herself over to her imaginings and the resulting forces that appear to surround her (near the end, she simply falls into the jutting arms protruding from the apartment walls), for she does step outside herself in a sense and accepts these forces as being just the way things are, detached and removed from her true self and state of being. She embodies the horror of losing control to the point where there is no escaping, acquiescing because she also can't understand. In *Repulsion*, where 'the (perceived) process of psychological disintegration in its protagonist has already begun, and is established as inevitable,' Carol's 'psychical developmental regression [is] a marker of her degenerating self' and she 'fails to identify herself within the realm in which she resides, [moving] closer toward this reconstruction' (Baker: 2018). Her inability to fully realize her own personality conforms to those in other Polanski features where the characters become, according to Helena Goscilo, citing Ann Lawton, 'non-beings [...] squeezed out of existence by the monsters that they themselves produce," their spiritual nullity captured by their "being cinematically frozen into a lifeless image"' (Orr/Ostrowska: 27).

Throughout several of Polanski's films, his characters are in a near constant state of anxious paranoia. They 'obsess over being watched and talked about' and 'invariably take the sound of muffled voices heard through shared walls to be threats, the beginnings of plots against them' (Wojtas). Indeed, there is often a subsequent 'Kafkaesque' plunge into madness where nothing is what it seems and the primary characters, subject to this condition, are themselves manipulated in order to deal with the apparent madness, accepting the world for what it appears to be or acting out in defiance. Carol is something of both. 'By utilizing characters who are in a state of nervous exhaustion to begin with,' notes McKibbin, 'Polanski suggests this off-screen time, and then manipulates minimal off-screen space [...] to create the necessary horror effects by other means, by more psychological means' (Orr/Ostrowska, 2006: 58). Furthermore, notes Baker, by 'Blurring the distinction between Carol's "imaginary realm and the diegetically real" as Caputo observes, in each of the three sequences in which Carol is brutally raped all diegetic sound, including her screams, is muted, as the same ticking heard during Hélène's [sic] intercourse infiltrates the scene.' In this confusion of what is reality and what is Carol's hallucination,' Baker notes how the viewer is 'immersed within, and forced to witness the brutality of her rape, her terrified expression obscured by the rapists' dirty fingers spread over her face, after which she wakes up alone and all sound is restored' (2018). Aural amplification (or the lack thereof) often works for Polanski in tandem with a sweeping atmosphere of psychological and tonal unease and the physical countenance of associated anxiety, from the same eerie silence heard in *Macbeth* to the 'expression of melancholy' described on the face of young Oliver Twist, from the mingling of the absurd and the unsettling in *What?* (hardly a horrific film but still taking place in a house with a symbolic life of own thanks to its ragtag inhabitants) to *Cul de sac*, where a sometimes-exhausting amalgam of tension and bleak, semi-comic behavior comingles with sexual tension and violent intimidation. In these films and elsewhere, as Morrison argues, 'The most comic moments in Polanski's films, as well as the most horrific, occur when some inner dimension of consciousness or some internal effect manifests itself on the surface, is made flesh, suddenly, palpably, and potently.' Polanski's 'most basic point seems to be that, especially after the worst has already happened, this is the fate of all subjectivity' (2007: 49).

AN EMPATHETIC CONNECTION

Somewhat appropriating the viewer's own engagement with Carol, the other characters in *Repulsion* likewise attempt and regularly fail to come to terms with what is plaguing Carol, to understand why she behaves the way she does. (For his part, Colin even struggles to express his own feelings, telling Carol after he barges into her apartment that he's 'not really like this, you know' and admitting he simply can't find the proper words.) Their inability to do so further contributes to the awful premonition of something within her being beyond the norms of straightforward understanding. She is a 'monstrous enigma' (Orr/Ostrowska: 123), but what differentiates the depiction of psychosis in *Repulsion* from films like *Psycho*, Michael Powell's *Peeping Tom* (1960) and Hitchcock's *Marnie* is, for Caputo, 'the film's *lack* of diegetic psychoanalyses and the attempt to represent, rather than merely include, the perceptual crises experienced by the film's protagonist' (2012: 84). Carol attempts to communicate her feelings and what may be troubling her ('I don't feel ... I mean ... I don't know'), perhaps intimating some acknowledgement of knowing instability, and she does, early on, continue to basically function at work, even showing concern for a crying friend ('Don't be upset,' she offers with a kindly, empathetic smile) and laughing as that same friend recalls and mimics Charlie Chaplin's *The Gold Rush* (1925), both instances that prove she is not wholly removed from the emotions of others. Yet just as swiftly, as swiftly as she abruptly turns her head and looks to the ground in the middle of a conversation, she reverts back to her vulnerable, frail and fragile self, combustible and inarticulate.

If 'Roman Polanski's *Repulsion* is a film as much about perspective as it is about paranoia,' as Aaron Hendrix has argued, it seems fitting, then, that 'its opening image—an extreme close-up of an eyeball—asserts as much from the very start.' 'In this sense,' Hendrix adds, 'the film's keen focus on perspective is operating on two levels: one, as a peek into the

Fig. 16. Sharing a laugh.

mind of a woman descending into madness, and, two, as an exploration of sexuality as viewed from youth' (Hendrix). The emphasis on eyes has regularly received due attention, in *Repulsion* and in films throughout the history of the medium, as arguably the most prominent vessel for identification and a cue for entering the complex states of associated anxiety. 'Eyes,' writes Stephen Prince, 'especially their wounding [...] are capable of provoking intense dread and anxiety, and in their gelatinous state, neither solid nor liquid, they form an uncertain, easily permeable barrier against the outside world' (2004: 122). In the horror film in particular, where 'perspective is key,' perception is 'played with, as in *The Shining* [Stanley Kubrick, 1980] and *Rosemary's Baby*, it is shifted, as in *Psycho*, and it is dissolved, as in *Repulsion*.' Perspective, notes Hendrix, 'carries the key to empathetic connection with the victim. But, ultimately, it is a tool used to come to grips with the terror that is unfolding on-screen, and, ideally, used to reach the catharsis toward which a horror film builds' (Hendrix). Certainly, as Clover also comments, while noting that the opening eye of horror is 'far more often an eye on the defense than an eye on the offense' (2015: 191), a standard moment in horror is 'one in which a person is caught by surprise—her vision assaulted—by the sight of things she does not want to see' (2015: 192). Influenced by Professor R. L. Gregory's *Eye and Brain: The Psychology of Seeing*, a text Polanski said 'lent scientific confirmation to many of the ideas [he'd] instinctively believed in since [his] film-school days—for instance, on the subject of perspective, size constancy, and optical illusions' (Polanski, 1985: 254), much of the director's resulting cinema, as Orr writes, 'thus depends on the art of perceiving and its multiple layering. Within his narrative there is always a key encounter between the strange and the familiar' (Orr/Ostrowska, 2006: 11).

However, despite this predominance of imagery associated with the eye and by association the act of seeing, little of *Repulsion* is actually seen via Carol's vantage; that is, the camera seldom adopts her point of view. Remaining on the outside, witnessing what happens as if it were truly occurring, point of view shots are limited as Polanski instead opts for what Caputo calls a camera 'tethered' to the protagonist, resulting in "'a visual style in which we, as spectators, are connected to a single character within the diegesis, rather than roaming through diegetic space to watch action that takes place between a variety of characters.'" The viewer, for the most part, "'observes the action of the film not from some extra-diegetic point of privilege (i.e., behind a fourth wall), but from somewhere within the diegetic space.'" Although we "'experience the film by way of Carole […] we are not Carole'" and she is "'more the object of our voyeuristic gaze than she is an on-screen surrogate'" (Quoted in Moore: 2016). At times, due in part to the emotional detachment discussed earlier, our primary identification is 'with the camera, wherever it may be and whatever it may be up to,' while our secondary identification is 'with the character of empathic choice.' Because of this, and because 'both are fluid,' as Clover writes, 'the camera can entertain different positions with ease—not just character positions, but omniscient ones—and with different degrees of "personality"' (2015: 8). As Polanski centers on Carol as she is caught up in some inexplicable dream-like trance, it's difficult to discern her internalized elucidation, compared to the subjective, hallucinatory stances employed during such moments as the rape sequences, where even still it is relatively hard to assume her precise emotional state. It is 47 minutes into the film when we hear the first crack in Carol's apartment wall, but we don't actually see the crack appear, only her reaction, so there is no telling if it has indeed been there all along or if this is just the beginning of her breakdown. Not long after, in any case, is when the mysterious male figure briefly appears in the mirror. And just a few minutes after that is when there is the first active crack, which is promptly followed by the first fantasy rape. For Carol, what may have been relatively nascent to begin with has begun in full, and still, even after her traumatic nocturnal assaults, she is often seen the morning after simply going about her daily routine. So, as Carol makes her way throughout her apartment with routine, disconcerting regularity, disinterested or distracted (either of which would suggest conscious mental activity), it is difficult, as Butler notes, 'to account for the powerful influence these wanderings, often photographed in large close-ups, have in drawing us closer to her, in helping us, so to speak, to "know" her' (1972: 153). Compare this technique to the astonishing dream sequence of *Rosemary's Baby*, where we are deeply embedded in the tortures of Rosemary's psyche. Here, writes Moore, 'we are able to stay within the confines of Rosemary's consciousness, knowing and suspecting no more than she does, and to share as much of this private and terrible experience as we can bear – and as Rosemary can bear.' The process is far more visceral, though no more potent, than the process of identification with Carol, even if the sequence 'better captures the horror of Rosemary's violation than simply showing a woman being attacked, objectively or subjectively, possibly could' (2016).

But as a 'portrait of neurosis, or psychosis, or mental illness,' the validity of *Repulsion* has led some to cast doubt on its representation in terms of clinical accuracy (Moore distrusts that 'many people go crazy this way' and questions if it is truly 'a way of turning Carole into someone who is alien, whom we can understand and feel compassion for but not relate to' [2016]) and reasoning, as Caputo opines when noting Carol's 'increasingly dangerous and bizarre' behavior and how the 'temptation to speculate as to the cause of her mental illness grows accordingly' (2012: 107). This temptation is thwarted considerably throughout *Repulsion*, certainly more so than in other Polanski films where prior trauma is more obvious and associative. Take *Death and the Maiden*, with its firm, jarring backstory (however uncertain to start) and its integration of committed memory to induce lingering trauma, which still doesn't prevent the other two parties involved from thinking Paulina is crazy based solely on the way she acts out what they see as paranoid delusions of persecution. When Paulina extinguishes candles as a car pulls up in the driveway and instinctively grabs a gun and locks herself in, the continuous practice suggests a preparation or at least an anticipation of some eventual threat. Also, in non-Polanski features already mentioned for their striking parallels, there is *The Haunting of Julia*, where Julia's torment is derived from understandable origins and the supernatural elements only later take the film in another direction. And as opposed to Thana in *Ms. 45*, who is appalled by her own acts and the incidents and her reactions haunt her dreams, and Mary in *Carnival of Souls*, who calls herself a 'reasonable person' and a 'a realist' and is aware of both the oddities plaguing her and how fantasies can 'get out of hand' in the dark, Carol is, on the whole, simply, chillingly, oblivious, attending to her sewing the day after one rape sequence as if life simply goes on. Even the bewildered, terrified Carrie attempts and ultimately seizes control when reaching her breaking point. Conversely, Carol seems like an otherwise normal young woman, and without the evident explanation of what causes her torment, it is at once challenging to fathom the unexplained, apparent randomness of her torment and it opens up the terrifying possibility of something far-reaching and applicable to anyone. Sitting by as we witness Carol's incremental decline, Caputo states that in *Repulsion*, 'the deepest source of horror is not the violence perpetrated on or by Carole, but our empathy with her growing alienation from the world; this horror comes from the fear not only that such a thing could happen to us, but the realisation that it may not be something than can be cured or even explained' (2012: 112).

ATTEMPTING TO UNDERSTAND

Witnessing the apparent innocuousness of what sets Carol off, the viewer of *Repulsion* is apt to scrutinize her reactions in order to ascertain some sort of reasoning, even if reason hardly figures into the equation. She appears surprised by her distorted kettle reflection, yet moves in closer, then turns back from it: Is she sensing something in the distortion, recognizing her progressively altered state? There are hints of abuse, perhaps, maybe even an incestuous assault or some other form of sexual disturbance, given her apparent aversion to sexuality. But when Carol rebuffs her sister's boyfriend, who derisively refers to her as 'Cinderella' and states how 'strung up' she is, her sister counters that she is just sensitive. She should, in any case, according to Michael, see a doctor. Such comments inaugurate the evidence of Carol's mental illness but still reduce what ails her to something as equivocal as being merely 'sensitive.' Due in part to her admittedly detached nature, there is with most who come into contact with Carol an inability to sympathize with her and what so obviously tortures her, or to see something deeper looming within her troubled psyche. While she stares at an untouched meal of fish and chips as if it evokes something far more than merely an unappetizing course, the sight of the food simply disgusts Colin, which suggests early on the ways in which different people will perceive different objects and react in accordance to their own interpretation. Similarly, when Carol first comments to Helen, 'We must get this crack mended,' Helen asks 'What?' before her attention is diverted elsewhere and the conversation stops (did she not hear or does she not know what Carol is talking about?). Through Polanski's 'transformation of claustrophobic settings into psychic space' (Orr/Ostrowska, 2006: 23), as is seen in several of his films, even with the proximity we are granted with Carol, we, as viewers, can never really diagnose Carol or say with certainty what past traumas befell her, so one can only imagine how those not privy to such personal moments may interpret her behavior.

Fig. 17. The origins of something lurking.

Although the camera picks up a family photograph several times, zooming back into a close shot of Carol's eye at the end of the film, adding further, final weight to the image of a clearly distressed Carol as a young girl, there is no indication of what is distressing her, at the moment of the photo's taking or previously in her young life. *Repulsion* is, as Orr writes, 'Enigmatic to the end […] The horror of the film [lying] in the wrong kind of transition, in rites of passage not from innocence to womanhood but from innocence to butchery' (Orr/Ostrowska, 2006: 13). Even so, having seen the ways in which Carol behaved throughout the film, there has been the proposition of some sort of childlike issue still plaguing her, suggested in her juvenile mannerisms and her stunted social interaction. 'The expression on the child's face is terrifying,' notes Butler, adding in what is certainly an understatement as it relates to *Repulsion*, 'and the more so for being inscrutable' (1972: 154). Nevertheless, Polanski wasn't particularly keen on exploring Carol's past or providing a reason for why she is like she is, opting instead for the indefinite depiction of her condition: 'I'm not very interested in whether Carole's [sic] disorder stems from her childhood, and contrary to some French critics, I didn't set out to make a Freudian film. I just stuck to describing someone whose motives are sometimes difficult to fathom' (Cronin, 2005: 9). Still, it is tempting to analyze the possibility, and Moore, for one, grapples with this related interpretation:

> I accept the reading of *Repulsion* as a film about a woman who was sexually abused as a child, as the final image of the family photo suggests, with its close-up of the child Carole's eyes, staring with demented hatred at the younger of the two adult men in the photo, presumably her father. In that case, her nightly visits may mingle fantasy with memories of visits from her father, and be an attempt to gain control over these memories, and reimagine the original events, by bringing them into line with her own desires. However, I paid little attention to this clue during my first several viewings of the film, since I didn't need it to make Carole's behaviour make sense to me. Whatever Carole's biography is supposed to be, the character works as a portrait of the profound contradictions, hypocrisy, and schizophrenia that is our cultural ideal of femininity and female sexuality. Having accepted that she must represent purity and innocence, she can only imagine sexuality as something alien and outside of her, something male, and sex as rape. The surreal contrast between Carole's outward childlike, blonde innocence and fragility and the lurid depravity of her fantasy life, not to mention the violence she's capable of, highlights how rotten the cultural ideal is in the first place' (2016).

Setting aside the possibility of her childhood trauma, there is no indication that Carol is otherwise exceptionally susceptible to any malevolent force, no more so, that is, than anyone else in or watching the film. 'It is astonishing that *Repulsion* neither forfeits sympathy for Carol nor tries to earn it with easy psychological explanations,' writes Morrison, 'refusing to minimize her own violence.' It is such that the film's empathy subsequently 'comes from its understanding of her repulsions, not its castigation of them, and we feel the intensity of her sense of violation, the reality of it, even as we recognize the rapes themselves as delusions' (2007: 34). This basic premise is central to the all-purpose effect of horror cinema, where regardless of how far-fetched or fantastical an event or character is, something integral in the very nature of most horror fare causes the viewer to go along with the process and identify with the narrative to the degree that even when it's a fantasy within the fantasy, such is the convincing and resounding quality of the picture that we feel the pain, the anxiety and the torment. 'But when the mind is the actual stuff of horror,' Butler contends, 'when madness and collapse are presented from inside, rather than viewed from without, then the solid ground itself shifts and crumbles, and we do indeed find ourselves looking into the bottomless pit. This is the fearful theme of *Repulsion*' (1972: 144).

CHAPTER 4: SETTING THE SCENE

As Carol moves carefully and woefully from room to room in her apartment, traversing its hallways with petrified trepidation, Polanski orchestrates external noises to signal a peripheral life outside, while inside, ticking clocks, buzzing flies and harassing phone calls form aural reminders of an animated domestic space, strengthening the abstract ambiance of her torment. 'As the film draws to its inevitable conclusion in the last fifteen minutes,' notes Hagen, and 'Carol's apartment becomes a full-on horror show of trashed furniture, a kitchen in total squalor, and two pesky corpses Carol has no way of disposing of,' she is 'literally pulled into the apartment in her state of extreme, male-driven paranoia' (2016). Leading to this point, though, Polanski's camera has scanned *Repulsion*'s interiors in a visual establishment of relevant decor, in Carol's apartment and elsewhere, often registered alongside tactile, abject textures (a pancake facial treatment or an untouched meal) and revolting objects like bloodstained floors, rotting potatoes and a decaying rabbit, the head of which finds its way to Carol's handbag, prompting the public revelation of her private disturbance. While this attention to tangible detail would be echoed in *The Tenant*, where Polanski's main character obsesses over clothes and trinkets and such grotesque items as a tooth stuck in a wall, signifying precursors to his mental break, the scenic establishment of Carol encased within the confining walls of her apartment also gestures toward the Polanski-esque pattern of a few characters in one combustible location, as recalled in chapter one, from the floating limitations of *Knife in the Water* and the violent intrusion of *Cul-de-Sac*, from the furtive stranger who enters the overwrought space of *Death and the Maiden* to the combative quartet within *Carnage*'s inhibited apartment.

PRODUCTION DESIGN

As he recalled in his autobiography, Polanski knew *Repulsion* would atmospherically 'stand or fall by the apartment where most of the action took place.' Together with art director Seamus Flannery, he 'built model of it on [his] living-room floor, making drawings wherever [his] English failed [him] during [their] detailed discussions.' His aim was to 'show Carol's hallucinations through the eye of the camera, augmenting their impact by using wide angle lenses of progressively increasing scope.' But in itself, he said, that wasn't sufficient for his purpose: 'I also wanted to alter the actual dimensions of the apartment—to expand the rooms and passages and push back the walls so that audiences could experience the full effect of Carol's distorted vision. Accordingly we designed the walls of the set so they could be moved outward and elongated by the insertion of extra panels. When "stretched" in this way, for example, the narrow passage leading to the bathroom assumed nightmarish proportions' (1985: 199). Because the film was a relatively low-budget endeavor and there was no special effects team, Polanski often handled the contraptions himself, acknowledging 'they took longer to set up than expected. The simplest hallucinations were the hardest to stage.' In the service of conveying Carol's disintegration via her surroundings, this included the 'replastering and repaint the cracks' and inserting a sprouting potato 'that marks the passage of time as Carol's mind slowly gives way,' something he says was borrowed straight from his childhood: 'It sprang from my recollection of the bean my grandmother had grown in her kitchen just before the war' (Polanski, 1985: 204). Realizing from the beginning where much of the film's thematic, visual, and dramatic thrust would gain its impact, 'the setting imposed itself before the story line crystallized' (Polanski, 1985: 231).

Stressing Carol's distorted sense of time and space, an expanding and retracting realm shaped by her perception, and as part of Polanski's formal approach to creatively deliver this depicted space as one of constant instability, lights are randomly seen on then off with no coherent cause and malleable clay-like walls become a visual cohesion with Carol's body. Influencing and influenced by her surroundings, a mutual manipulation with Polanski as a third-party authority, hallways become elongated and foreboding and the living room widens in distended fashion. As with *Rosemary's Baby* and *The Tenant*, the mystery of *Repulsion*'s horror exemplifies the ways in which a single character's mentality is fostered by the area that surrounds them, and vice-versa. 'The reality Polanski works in from film to film is mutable,' notes Wojtas, 'and the lines separating what takes place in and outside the minds of his characters are deliberately obscured. But each entry in the trilogy retains an unnervingly plausible strain of psychological realism, even when courting the supernatural' (Wojtas). What is reality and what is purely a figment of Carol's imagination would typically be delineated by point of view shots suggesting her subjective impression, but what of the angles seen in which Carol moves around as her projected anxieties take shape not just before her very eyes, but ours as well? Polanski's camera reveals an equally distorted atmosphere where the vantage is not taken from the one who presumably accounts for the distortion, yielding an imperiling atmosphere of unease and uncertainty and unlimited potential. It is only at the calamitous end when there appears, during the concluding reveal of what Carol has been up to during her sister's absence, a visual and narrative sense of returning to normalcy, as the skewed vision 'collapses down to a normal view when Helen, Michael, and the neighbors enter the apartment. They see things normally and, at that point, we do' (Holland).

Also shooting on a range of exterior locations, capturing the seemingly innocuous regular world and the goings on of an average day, Polanski lends *Repulsion* an initial, surface sense of reality, grounding the story's shell in an illustration of relative certainty—a life of regularity, a life 'out there.' From the bustling Vidal Sassoon beauty salon to the street scenes of people walking along the sidewalk, street musicians performing, nuns playing in the courtyard and people dining in restaurants, the establishment of a daily life going on as usual was crucial to Polanski, who felt it was important to surround Carol with normality to accentuate the extraordinary within her mind and her home. Yet it is a world riddled with threats and menace all the same, including, for Carol, aggressive, leering men and the omnipresent, seemingly ordinary objects that take on bizarre connotations to twist and inform her vivid, disturbed imagination. As noted early in the film, almost as a passing aside, this is a world that, for all its constancy, is nevertheless full of the incongruous and the uncanny, where eels are apparently emerging from sinks, an incident that receives minor mention but one which, in its weird essence, bears significant later repercussions, nodding to the notion that not only is there something odd brewing within Carol, but that what exists outside may be less typical that appearances might suggest. There is a subtle, prevalent strangeness that may, in fact, be feeding the sensations magnified by Carol's own psychological distortion. The outside world, in other words, may be nearly as horrific as Carol imagines. Similarly expressive external supplements occur at several points in *Rosemary's Baby*, where although the apartment doesn't so much take on a life of its own, as in *Repulsion*, it does become a representative shelter, an imprisoning confine detached from an outlying life going on around its unwitting victim, a life that includes mention of the Pope visiting New York City and the cover of Time Magazine asking 'Is God dead?', elements of cultural context and relevant inclusions in terms of the film's religious evocation.

Fig. 18. Elements of the abject.

Polanski in fact inserts elusive hints of uncertainty throughout the early portions of *Repulsion*, establishing tangential features that will only later assume a slanted place in Carol's unsound mind. The skinned rabbit, planned for an ultimately aborted meal, the chiming church bells, the accosting workman, the naturally worn cracks on the sidewalk: these elements present visual and aural cues and clues of what's to come, but do so, at first glance, out of the subsequent context that makes their existence so noteworthy. Most, including perhaps Carol (presumably prior to where the film picks up), would fail to see the signs that something potentially destructive is emerging. But as 'violence disrupts the world of everyday life' and 'explodes our assumptions about normality,' as Isabel Cristina Pinedo writes, the subsequent horror is indeed 'produced by the violation of what are tellingly called natural laws—by the disruption of our presuppositions about the integrity and predictable character of objects, places, animals, and people' (Prince: 91). These signifiers *will* gradually form to a further, exaggerated extent within Carol's apartment, where the literal restriction and her innate vulnerability increases the capacity for auxiliary concern. Terror itself, or at the very least these indicators of embryonic terror, is therefore 'within and without' according to Sandford (2008, 82). It surely exists, but the importance and the conclusive menace is housed entirely within the inaccessible mind of Carol herself, producing an atmospheric strain that is a direct result of, or at any rate bears a direct correlation to, the setting's literal makeup or a single character's perception. In this way, *Repulsion* has often been linked to Robert Wise's *The Haunting* (1963), where Julie Harris' Eleanor Lance appears as arguably the primary vessel through which the haunted abode expresses its malicious potential. It 'does not mean that the haunting itself is explained away as a mere projection of Eleanor's precarious mental state,' however, as Peter Hutchings writes.'In fact the whole film is predicated on the idea of Hill House being haunted prior to Eleanor's arrival' (2004, 73). Still, one can't help but relate the goings on and the repeated mention of the house being a living, breathing, even thinking entity, a house that was 'born bad,' a house that is alive, that has patience, that is sick and crazy and deranged, and attributing that acuity, with *Repulsion*-esque significance, to the echoing of what plagues the unsound Eleanor, who suffers from her own childhood trauma and routinely has her sanity questioned. Returning to *Nightmare on Elm Street*, certainly an appropriate comparison concerning the depiction of horror's dream-to-reality overlap, Pinedo alludes to postmodern scenes where 'the referent or "reality" is gone,' and the main character is 'caught within a closed system from which there is no exit. It is thus that the postmodern horror genre operates on the principle of undecidability.' In Carol's fluctuating dream state, a state from which there appears no evasion even when she is awake, questions emerge regarding what will save the young woman, what can she do when she is trapped in such a confined context that may or may not be entirely of her own conception, what is her saving grace and what is the true monster to be combatted? *Repulsion* carries with it an increasing sense of inevitable dread because the film does not obey the formulaic notions of traditional good and evil, nor does it explain away its terror in any concrete form. 'This principle is extended from the narrative level to the cinematographic level,' notes Pinedo, aligning Polanski's film with postmodern horror and its tendency to repeatedly blur the 'boundary between subjective and objective representation by violating the conventional cinematic (lighting, focus, color, music) codes that distinguish them' (Prince: 94).

Reflecting and affecting her fears, the Kensington flat Carol shares with Helen, constructed in Twickenham studios, is a palpable expression of anxiety, realized primarily in Polanski's illustrative production design. The apartment appears in a perpetual state of flux, a cumulative disarray that parallels Carol's debilitating breakdown and evolves the apartment to such a degree that it communicates any number of horrific surprises.

Filmmakers, as Hutchings writes, 'will do whatever they can to get past our defences, either using areas of off-screen space that we might not have thought of as dangerous (above and below the frame, for example, rather than at the sides) or through increasing the volume of sound associated with the startle' (2004, 140). And surely here, aural allusions of footsteps and other nerve-wracking noises unite with alternating casts of illumination and exaggerated structural fractures, pliable walls and a room suddenly and without reason magnified, coalescing in a disorienting spatial and temporal construction where 'time is marked by the ticking of a clock rather than by a play of sunlight and darkness' (Horrigan: 2009). Combating the escalation of terror as her illusions grow more severe and more frequent, Carol retreats inward and shuts out more of the world, a visibly disarming degeneration into further madness as blinds are drawn to add to the air of stifling heat, restriction and tension. As the film nears its conclusion and Carol's instability has been amplified, any potential configuration of herself and the setting, which may 'come alive' at any moment, yields a terrifying revelation of scenic variability. And once wholly isolated, the film exits out of time, a disconcerting interval where abjection looms like 'one of those violent, dark revolts of being, directed against a threat that seems to emanate from an exorbitant outside or inside, ejected beyond the scope of the possible, the tolerable, the thinkable' (Kristeva, 1982: 1). In Polanski's films, Morrison states, 'though the things of the objective world provide a full complement of possibilities to obscure—behind, beyond, beneath, within—their eerie transparency remains their most striking feature' (2007: 67), and it becomes as Julia Kristeva describes, where 'it is thus not lack of cleanliness or health that causes abjection but what disturbs identity, system, order. What does not respect borders, positions, rules' (1982: 4). The positioning of these elements often where they shouldn't be, transgressing these borders, is such that for all of his brutality and despicableness, the landlord isn't far off when he calls the apartment a 'flaming nut house.' Unlike *The Fearless Vampire Killers*, where the interior design is rife with traditional elements of horror cinema—creaking doors, cobwebs and coffins—nor like the profusive religious symbolism of *Carrie* or the home left behind in *The Haunting of Julia*, where the house would only serve as a traumatic reminder of Julia's deceased daughter, *Repulsion*'s interior accoutrements are simply commonplace elements that, when taken outside of Carol's perception, appear relatively banal. 'A similar argument has already been formulated by David Hume,' notes

Laine, 'who stated that the negative emotions in an aesthetic experience could be overcome by the delight of the artistic expression that overwhelm and absorb them, instead of simply cancelling them out (Hume 2007). In *Repulsion*, the opposite is true: the disgust-horror it evokes works concertedly to overwhelm this kind of appreciation, but in spite of this we stay with the film.' In *Repulsion*, which imposes 'an emotional effect upon the spectator by means of its aesthetic patterns of salience, which enable the spectator to "tune in" to the disgust-horror that the film embodies. [...] it is the film's aural, visual, and haptic textures which terrorize us in a manner similar to the immaterial presence that terrorizes Carole in the street' (2011).

Fig. 19. *Cracks in the interior signal the cracks of Carol's psyche.*

POLANSKI'S TECHNIQUE

In terms of its jarring camera movements, its multilayered sound design, its canted angles and intense close-ups, special effects and skewed subjectivity, *Repulsion* is one of the more audaciously stylish of Roman Polanski's films. And yet, a sullen camera will often hold on Carol as she lies down or sits and stares, the relative inaction triggering the sensation of impending discord while the stress on concentrated stillness and silence induces a slow burn decline into psychosis; similarly, Polanski's camera will wander in meditative tracks and pans before scenes end in slow fades to black, prodding the mounting pressure by way of wearing down the surface permanency to uncover an ingrained horror. And as Carol's edgy, deliberate movements are bolstered by duration, her descent illustrated in distorted imagery, irregular focal lengths, wide lenses and low angles, a stress on technique rarely seen in Polanski's later films, he also embraces common horror practice by teasing imminent jeopardy, providing the viewer with knowledge characters don't have (the unsuspecting landlord who accosts Carol as she stands with the razor blade behind her back for only us to see), and infuses the picture with such characteristically frightening scares as the unaccountable male figure glimpsed in a flash and the violent release of Carol as she slashes wildly at her victims or pummels them without mercy, the dark black blood splatter intensified by a discordant assembly of sounds. 'For the (presumably) sane spectator,' Caputo remarks, such contrasts in stylistic representation 'are both disquieting and fascinating in that they draw attention to the relative malleability of (or perception of) what we cling to as being essentially immutable external realities. Conversely, if the distorting effects are limited by careful camera placement, Polanski maintains that a wide-angle lens can also serve to heighten the illusion of depth' (2012: 38). Despite numerous moments of 'raw, avant- garde ingenuity,' though, as Wojtas comments, 'the bulk of *Repulsion* is dominated by careful compositions, considered camera movements and long takes of Carol just existing, unraveling.' What other 1960s horror film, he wryly and wisely observes, would have predicted Chantal Akerman's *Jeanne Dielman, 23 Commerce Quay, 1080 Brussels* (1975), a masterful, methodical exploration of femininity within a stolid domestic space (Wojtas). Touches of household familiarity have also been seen in several of the aforementioned films with notable resemblances to Repulsion. There is, for example, the bathtub or shower as a place to recover (*Carrie* and *I Spit on Your Grave*), to kill and dispose of a body (*I Spit on Your Grave* and *Ms. 45*) and as a place to suggest the ultimate vulnerability (*Psycho* and *Carnival of Souls*). These films, like *Repulsion*, take notions of the home as the ultimate safe space and thwart those associations by presenting a place where even conceivably friendly figures (Colin, for example, or Farrow's estranged husband in *The Haunting of Julia*) are perceived as, or genuinely are, threatening personages. Similar violations are also seen in Polanski's *The Ghost Writer* and *Frantic*, where mystery hangs over the entirety of both films after supposedly safe spaces are invaded by outside actors. 'Reaffirming the trauma of dislocation central to Polanski's work,' Baker notes how the 'decay and subsequent unfamiliarity of Carol's apartment relates to Freud's articulation of the uncanny,' which he figures through an analogy of the home.

> Signifying that which is simultaneously strangely familiar yet alien, Freud writes that "the unheimlich [uncanny] is what was once heimisch, homelike, familiar; the prefix "un" is the token of repression." It is precisely the evocation of the home in Carol's trauma, which exacerbates her pathological repression, as her fear of sex is channelled through violent fantasies of seduction, which take place in her increasingly unfamiliar home. (2018)

Such invasions are all the more significant in cases of a female, particularly a lone female, victim, where the correlation between the woman and the house forges a symbolic, extra-textual parallel. As Harrington writes:

> Reading the metaphorical use of houses as proxies for women's minds and bodies in horror films is troubling when considering the discursive positioning of the woman's corporeal body—her "house"—as a space and place for man. However, such spatial analogies are particularly sinister in *Rosemary's Baby* and *Demon Seed* [Donald Cammell, 1977], which deal with rape, coercion and forced pregnancies. It is the women's bodies, more than the physical houses, which are invaded (2018: 101).

In canvassing the area that surrounds Carol, Polanski not only covers the fantastical elements born from her imagination, but he adorns the scene, the apartment especially, with realistic, everyday elements to portend her state of mind and the passage of time, forming an oftentimes surreal pattern of decor where 'objects become signifiers of Carol's mental erosion' (Baker: 2018). The interplay of these objects, what they signify to Carol and to the viewer, how they develop, devolve or are simply moved about, suggests a perpetual state of unease and transgression. From her vehement application of lipstick to the way she scratches at a non-existent something on glass, 'Carol's fascination with peripheral objects may derive from some awareness of her own marginality, and the attentions she gives them requite the attentions she herself rarely receives, and which she repels when she does' (Morrison, 2007: 143). This is seen in the predominance of graphic textures throughout the film, particularly food and drink in various stages of consumption and especially that skinned rabbit, emerging in the first act, as Greenberg notes, like 'Chekhov's Gun [...] a barometer of Carole's sanity' and an indication of time's passing, which as noted earlier is often indeterminate (2013: 55). Of the prevalence of food imagery, a psychoanalytic critic would 'point to oral themes: food, disgust, confusion of boundaries [and how] these are consistent with schizophrenia' (Holland). Even the eating scene from *The Gold Rush*, which Carol's coworker describes, features Chaplin turning into a chicken in the eyes of his starving companion, introducing, as Norman Holland point out, 'yet another eating metaphor,' a scene that, like *Repulsion*, 'projects the characters' interior thoughts into visible objects on screen' (Holland). The pervasiveness of food and drink (food loathing being 'perhaps the most elementary and most archaic form of abjection,' according to Kristeva [1982: 2]) similarly appears in Polanski's *What?* and *Tess*, in the perversity and sensuality of textures relating to consumption, in *Death and the Maiden* (Paulina's husband eating chicken out of the trash) and in *Oliver Twist*, with plates of slop slurped by starving scavengers. Alluding to *Rosemary's Baby*, which has its own fair share of unappealing and narratively ominous food placement, Morrison notes that when Polanski is 'deprived of the inwardness of metaphor,' his 'images become figures made flesh, gross substance retaining vestiges of its significance as symbol but mainly notable for its corporeality as brute matter—slabs of meat, like the rotting rabbit in *Repulsion* or the bloody livers rosemary gobbles in *Rosemary's Baby*' (2007: 131).

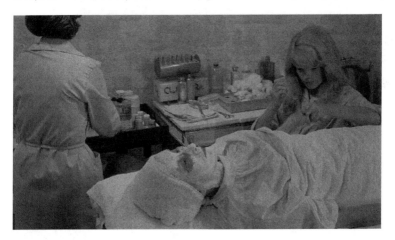

Fig. 20. Textures that are harsh, unnatural and foreboding.

The opening setting of *Repulsion*, 'at first glance a hospital operating theatre or some ghastly horror-film torture chamber' (Butler, 1970: 74), shows an elderly woman receiving a facial treatment, the image of cracked, dried and coarse textures appearing unpleasant and unrefined, harsh and unnatural. But the choice of a manicurist is not accidental for Ewa Mazierska, who sees the occupation as one 'whose job is to look after somebody else's hands [which] can be seen as particularly prone to mix subject with object' (2007: 37). Items of correspondingly ominous significance proliferate the duration of *Repulsion* as well as much of Polanski's succeeding work, including the first appearance of the sharp tweezers in Carol's salon, anticipating the blood that sure enough comes (accompanied by a blood-curdling scream) and Helen's black glove as her surreptitious hand enters the frame to wake Carol, as well as the charm necklace in *Rosemary's Baby* and the cigarettes, hieroglyphs and the dresser of clothing in *The Tenant*, all of which become relevant in terms of Trelkovsky's personality shift. Polanski's films are thus effusive with images and objects that not only bear narrative relevance but are in themselves significant thematic and visual signifiers of emotion and, oftentimes, sinister dread: *The Ninth Gate* (the hanging body; the deceased baroness, her tongue hanging out; the pentagrams; the mysterious book itself); *The Ghost Writer* (the dead former writer's clothes; his body washed ashore; the manuscript—'It was the book that killed him' says the new writer's agent); *Chinatown* (Jake's bandaged, bloody nose; the flaw in Evelyn's iris); *Bitter Moon* (an assortment of bodily fluids); *Carnage* (vomit); *Oliver Twist* (the grotesque makeup of Kingsley's Fagin). Even *Frantic* conveys 'most of the expected Polanski trademarks […] well in evidence, beginning with the growing sense of unease which can be inspired by relatively minor incidents—what Victorian ghost story writer M R James referred to as "the malice of inanimate objects"' (Meikle, 2006: 259). 'For Polanski,' Greenberg notes, 'the devil has always been in the details. He understands that little things can be as horrific as cutting off heads. *Repulsion* is full of these small touches that make it come to life' (2013: 55).

NO PAST, ONLY PRESENT

Given there is no preexisting explanation for what ails Carol, and given the fact that even as the film continues to unfold there is little that actually happens not relating to

Carol's gradual breakdown in the present tense, *Repulsion* is, in this sense, as Horrigan notes, a film where 'there is no past' (2009), where everything seen is in the disjointed moment. Put another way, '*Repulsion* is without plot [...] a series of virtuosic set-pieces interspersed with scenes of Carole going through slightly unhinged versions of her daily routine' (Moore: 2016). With a score composed by jazz musician Chico Hamilton and with measured editing by Alastair McIntyre (who edited six of Polanski's films), *Repulsion* is a jarring combination of manic energy and stately progression. It is, as Sandford critiques, 'more deliberately paced (among numerous other distinctions) than today's standard slasher flick [letting] us know how susceptible its heroine is, not just to criminal insanity, but to the full spectrum of neuroses' (2008: 82-83). Indeed, Polanski's intended sense of pacing, especially the rhythm of the early part of the film, was a sticking point when it came to selling the picture to producers Klinger and Tenser. Writing in his autobiography, Polanski stated, 'The first fifteen minutes of *Repulsion* were purposefully conceived as a buildup to that sickening split second when Carol has her first real hallucination—when she suddenly glimpses, reflected in the mirror on the wardrobe doors as it swings shut, a menacing male figure in the corner of her room. The shock effect, which had filmgoers jumping out of their seats, required a deliberately low-key approach' (1985: 205-206). Realized not only through its steadily unnerving pace, the peripheral sounds and sporadic lack of music give *Repulsion* what could aptly be described as a razor's edge tension. The dripping faucet and ticking clock, dogs barking, her sister in the throes of passion: all are amplified in an aural exaggeration, providing sonic cues to Carol's progressive breakdown. At the same time, the inflated nature of these sounds are further instances of Polanski infusing the film with subjective traits that prompt uncertainties regarding the authenticity of more drastic occurrences. The viewer's perception is continually predicated on Carol's vantage and our tenuous association with her perspective. Furthermore, the film expresses a systematic approach to the film's horror, sometimes at odds with the quick and dirty (however effective) processes of low-budget genre fare, as Cwik notes concerning *Carnival Of Souls* and how Polanski expounds on that 'shoestring classic' by using 'heightened sounds and simple, articulate camerawork to compensate for budgetary restrictions,' creating an 'oppressive atmosphere' (2015). Forging past certain budgetary and scenic limitations, Polanski's vision in *Repulsion* is indeed one emboldened by technique, by carefully arranged inserts, movements and juxtapositions, most of which are in the service of translating the inner wrangling of its central protagonist.

Fig. 21. An outbreak of violence.

The slow burn nature of the film's opening passages is also why the violence is so shocking when it comes in such rapid, unexpected bursts. Polanski conveys Carol's fear and anxiety in an intrepid combination of technical assembly and performance, with cryptic quick cuts to her eye and her problematically realized sensitivity to violence, oblivious to a car accident one moment, absolutely appalled by a trickle of blood the next. During the murder scenes especially, Polanski submits a vast range of technique and reaction. It's not Colin's twitching hand nor the blood splattering on the door that distresses Carol upon bashing her would-be boyfriend, after which she casually sits back down the candlestick holder (Polanski used a bicycle pump and his 'secret formula' for blood: cochineal and Nescafe [Polanski, 1985: 206]), but the drops of blood cascading from his head that sets her off. And then, in response to this, she frantically wipes away the blood with a nearby book and begins to board the broken door shut. Is it the mess that abhors her, which would be curious given the general state of the apartment, or is she attempting to remove evidence of the murder, which would also be odd as it would suggest a knowledge on her part that she has indeed committed a misdeed? The apparent premeditation of the landlord's murder is also complicated by the conflicting interpretations of her cognizance (a third murder, ultimately scrapped for the film, had Carol killing Michael's wife, an act deemed too reasonable for such an otherwise unreasonable woman). Moore explores in detail the visual, tonal and thematic complexity of the landlord's razor slaying:

> Whereas the murder of Colin is the absurd end of a clod [...] the landlord's murder is more satisfying: he's older, and his slight portliness suggests animalism and adds to the whiff of economic exploitation and class war, and he actually attacks her, climbing on top of her on the couch. Polanski, however, has Carole's razor attack go on for so long that we're brought around again from satisfaction to horror and sympathy: we occupy the victim's point of view (or the camera does: the landlord himself has his eyes screwed shut in agony) as Carole bends over him, darting in for little slices, her expression horrified but determined and curious, like she's conducting an experiment on something non-human (like her experiment with the beauty salon client's cuticle). Bits of black blood sully her white dress and her spun-sugar hair. The comic image of the blonde Victorian child-woman, her purity and beauty fouled with the blood of her murder victim, an amoral doll so persuaded of her perfect innocence that she's unaware of her own power to harm, is, for me, *Repulsion*'s crowning deconstruction of this particular cultural ideal of femininity. (2016)

The incremental danger Polanski maintains throughout *Repulsion* breeds a stately, nameless, unidentifiable dread that emerges from its ambiguity. Carol registers varying degrees of panic and tolerance; she appears nervous and fearful but is generally seen with a perpetually inscrutable, remote expression. And it is frequently this, her lack of response, which is so unnerving. The fear isn't so much in what is happening, but in what is she going to do next and how will she react, an anticipatory primer that keeps the film's tension at a nearly constant strain. 'Is Carole's experience of sensory overload in the hallway as she's caressed by disembodied male hands representative of the kind of effect Polanski would have liked to achieve with his cinema?' wonders Moore.

> Failing that, Polanski turns his attention [...] to transmitting tactile sensations, odors, and visceral experiences to the viewer through visual attention to texture and to disgust-evoking sights. Instead of concentrating disgust in a single figure of horror, Polanski ensures that throughout *Repulsion*, we, like Carole, feel low-level queasiness

punctuated by crisis moments of sudden, acute disgust. […] We may not be Carole, but we have been made, through Polanski's evoking of sensations, to understand something about how Carole experiences the world (2016).

The unceasing manipulation of Carol's apartment thus leaves open the potential for any new development, yielding the horrific tension of anything being possible and coming from any direction, of inanimate objects and their potential for destruction, of her own fear and of the perception of fear itself.

CONCLUSION

Fig. 22. Genre or something more?

An open ending and Polanski's intended ambiguity made *Repulsion* a psychological thriller that exceeded the norms of what he deemed a cheap horror film. But while the movie was greeted with generally positive appraisal, Polanski himself still viewed the production as 'an artistic compromise' (1985: 207), deriding its technical qualities in particular. Still, there can be no denying *Repulsion*'s subsequent reputation within the horror genre, as a unique feature in its own right—advanced in many ways, especially in its psychological acuity—and as it aligns with related horror precursors, from *Psycho* to the similarly low-budget, atmospheric work of Val Lewton. Or, as Bill Horrigan notes, nodding to another horror staple, the atmosphere of Carol's apartment is 'sketched with a flair for shock and showmanship that would be fully at home in a classic horror movie like *The Old Dark House* (1932), a useful reminder that Polanski has always embraced, if only to upend, the pleasures of genre filmmaking' (2009). Which is true, for however much he may have looked down upon the horror film generally (probably less than he liked to submit), Polanski knew the rules of the game, and in *Repulsion*, he managed to adapt his unique sense of scenic configuration, tension, timing and characterization to form one of the genre's most unique and outstanding entries. In doing so, and perhaps there was never any other way, Polanski imbued in the film an assortment of his trademark gestures, many of which, as has been discussed, would be most apparent in the remaining two films of his Apartment Trilogy, films that would in many ways not only define Polanski's cinema at large, but would also establish his place in the annals of horror film history. 'Whilst Polanski's cinema seems to start in the realm of 'high' art,' as Caputo remarks, 'it tends to move towards popular genre, as if through his forced foray into the genre cinema with *Repulsion* [...] Polanski was able to realise his skill at delivering the Camp pleasures of genre. [...] it is in fact *Repulsion*, and not *Knife in the Water* or *Cul-de-sac*, which best predicts the aesthetic direction of his cinematic career' (2012: 58). Further, films like *Repulsion*, *Rosemary's Baby* and *The Tenant* would be forever linked to what befell Polanski's personal life in the years prior and those following, though this, as Meikle argues, is a tenuous connection: 'There is a limit to how far one can extrapolate the coincidence of these three narratives with events in Polanski life, especially when only the first of them was originated by him. But the attraction of such a dynamic to a director was confined as a boy in similarly Gothic apartments, while evil without was enacted alongside potential betrayal within [...] is undeniable.' And, as he adds, 'Polanski taking the central role of Trelkovsky only adds to this impression' (2006: 218).

Nevertheless, and with this in mind, just as this study began so too will it end with the acknowledgement that Roman Polanski's body of work, particularly those features that fall firmly or even loosely within the strictures of the horror genre, bear a prominent correlation with the life of the filmmaker himself, perhaps not in the actual events of his life, but at least his worldview or, as the case may be, in the many rumors and stories about his personal life. 'A Polanski film isn't just a self-contained aesthetic object,' Leaming justly observes, 'for it exists against the vivid background of the director's biographical legend' (1981: 205), and in the ensuing years, particularly those just before and after the Manson murders, the connection grew inseparable. 'The evil and violence of such Polanski films as *Repulsion*, *Rosemary's Baby*, *Macbeth* and *Chinatown* ran parallel to the terrors of his own life' (Kiernan, 1980: 9), so while some of these films may have derived from the work of another author, the connections are nevertheless prominent and revealing. As Leaming argues, regarding *Rosemary's Baby* specifically, 'Polanski had seen something irresistible in [Ira] Levin's book—himself. Although Levin later denied it, Polanski thought the novelist must have seen Repulsion and been influenced by it.

How otherwise account for his own feeling of familiarity?' (1981: 83) In any event, these films as well as *Repulsion* (even more so), are set apart from most modern movies, as Greenberg argues, noting how with *The Tenant*, it becomes 'impossible to tell what's going to happen next, which is what makes it so scary. And as an example of alienation and urban paranoia taken to an extreme, the film resonates with many of Polanski's past and future themes' (2013: 139).

Films like *Repulsion* also helped establish the prominence of something else that would be included in nearly all subsequent Polanski features, including those with 'no obvious link with the [horror] genre at all (*Death and the Maiden* and *The Pianist*), but still [having] much in common with the films that do, and even of the feelings generated by horror cinema' (Orr/Ostrowska, 2006: 54). For Polanski, while he reveled in and succeeded with genre movies, as Ehrenstein notes, 'just beneath they're something more,' and of the Apartment Trilogy in particular, he points to an overarching theme that would extend itself throughout Polanski's body of work, in various guises, positioning these films as 'thoroughgoing explorations of the terror, anxiety, and above all, ambivalence we have about the sinister, the occult, and the "unknown"' (2012: 19). There may be the instances of something like *The Fearless Vampire Killers*, complete with an MGM logo dripping blood and banking on more comic horror than *Repulsion*, integrating common tropes like howling wolves, debilitating garlic, vampires and a full moon, absurd exaggerated, illustrative lighting and shadow play and a fear hardly related to the audience in any threatening way, but even that integrates the critical Polanski juxtaposition between the horrific and the indefinite, the horrific and banal and the 'the horrific and the funny,' which is 'reminiscent of Polanski's short films and of *Cul-de-sac*, and prefigures *Macbeth* and later horror films by this director.' Although it is, in this way at least, typical of Polanski's cinema, *The Fearless Vampire Killers* is itself rare in the horror film, pioneering a new trend, as Mazierska notes, citing the comments of S.S. Prawer, 'characteristic of the 1970s, thanks to being open-ended and therefore "unsafe" to the viewer—as opposed to the earlier horror movies which tended to "jolt us out from our everyday life, transporting us into problem which are clearly not our own"' (2007: 170). *Macbeth* likewise allies with *Repulsion* in its depiction of temptation and torment and a threatening woman, of murderous vengeance and pervasive unease resulting in frenzied bloodshed. It has the nightmarish dread of 'full-blooded Gothic horror, long before the term was coined officially—a delirious descent into a whirlpool of treachery and deceit, blood and madness—yet Polanski's version is somehow constrained by its own potential for excess' (Meikle, 2006: 178). In such films, and surely *Repulsion* among them, one sees how Polanski takes the conventions of horror cinema, or at the very least horror imagery and themes, and integrates them to offer up a grander picture of the world at large, a world where 'evil in the hearts of men is not an abstract concept [and] the extreme behavior of Macbeth and his wife seems all too human' (Greenberg, 2013: 107). There are also the seductive powers of evil, comic, perverse and strange, as in *Bitter Moon* and *What?*, where in that latter film the peculiar events are enough to prompt a priest to remark on the 'evil pestilence' that seems to envelope its characters and their madhouse abode. *Death and the Maiden*, opening as it does 'on a dark and stormy night,' has 'some of the trappings of a horror movie, but the real horror here is human' (Greenberg, 2013: 187), while, conversely, in a way combining the two, *The Ninth Gate* is 'as sinister as any of Polanski's pictures' (Orr/Ostrowska, 2006: 17) with its range of threats both paranormal and entirely substantial, peculiar and shared globally. 'Although Polanski's cinema normally defuses any straightforward diagetic truth regarding the existence of the supernatural, *The Ninth Gate* joins *Dance of the Vampires* [original title of *The Fearless Vampire Killers*] in the presentation of dietetically unambiguous supernatural activity' (Caputo, 2012: 240). Even *The Pianist*, though hardly a horror film in the traditional sense, does 'touch base with [Polanski's] earlier sense of the uncanny in a specific way [moving] progressively from a cauldron of noise and bustle into silence and emptiness' (Orr/Ostrowska, 2006: 19), not unlike *Repulsion*, *The Fearless Vampire Killers*, *Rosemary's Baby* and *The Ninth Gate*. 'As viewers,' states Morrison, 'we are never permitted to inure ourselves to it or to prepare ourselves for the next incident because—like the violence represented in *Macbeth*—it comes always a shade more quickly than expected. Though each act of violence is portrayed in its full horror, a share of that horror comes from how like commemoration—namely, none—each death calls forth' (2007: 106).

'The gothic is not normally the source of Polanski's horror though often as in *Cul-de-Sac*, *The Fearless Vampire Killers* and *The Ninth Gate* it can be a vital accompaniment,' writes Orr, 'a source of his dark humour and his mockery. But normally horror emerges out the humdrum detail of everyday life' (Orr/Ostrowska, 2006: 19). Such is the horror of *Repulsion*, which heralds an enduring shift in Polanski's assessment of how horror functions, growing clearer and more elaborate as his work continued, advocating a different way to look back at the films that came before and the continued predominance of something graver and more wicked in his worldview. 'A filmmaker slightly beyond the horror genre,' Polanski works 'off psychology more than terror' (Orr/Ostrowska, 2006: 51), portending the horror that surrounds us all, and is thus apparent in so many of his film. It is often manifest in 'what Jewish political philosopher Hannah Arendt referred to as the "banality of evil" in relation to the crimes of Adolf Eichmann. The horror implicit in the prospect of acts of intimidation conducted by unsophisticated German "squaddies" who suddenly find themselves in a position to play God over a people who have been classified as less than human is well captured' (Meikle, 2006: 310). Even when there are those films—like those of the Apartment Trilogy—where the typical horror elements are front and center, there is more at play, a degree of universality that emboldens the links running throughout Polanski's filmography, the idea 'of a human being in a state of ill-ease menaced by something bigger than the moment' (Orr/Ostrowska, 2006: 53). In *Chinatown*, by no means a horror film, there is nevertheless 'a diabolic tissue more rooted, more actual, more ubiquitous than anything in *Rosemary's Baby*' (Orr/Ostrowska, 2006: 15), realized primarily in the sense of one's life spiraling out of life control, the fatalistic certainty that bad things will inevitably, eventually happen, the same sort of dread that looms large over *Repulsion* from start to finish and was likely informed by the traumas of Polanski's childhood (seen also in *Oliver Twist*'s relentlessly horrendous and demoralizing circumstances). *Macbeth*, the first film Polanski made after the death of Tate and their unborn child, is a profoundly, potently grim feature with conspiratorial plotting and the sights and sounds that induce a persistent paranoia, where evil is pervasive and comes in many guises, *a la Repulsion*. But in a larger view of this continual conflict between the good and bad, 'Evil and the Devil are two separate things,' comments Polanski, touching on a distressing ubiquity. 'The Devil is how humans often like to imagine evil, with horns and a tail. Evil is part of our personality' (Cronin, 2005: 175). His observations, routinely put into practice, support Robin Wood's assertion that 'the monsters in horror are expressions of social and psychological repression (with the two inextricably linked) [and] can reveal truths about the political and social structures within which we all live' (Hutchings, 2004: 38).

For Polanski, who claimed his agnosticism prevented him somewhat from banking too much on the religiousness of *Rosemary's Baby*, or the depiction of the demonic child at the end, preferring to leave things obscure and ambiguous, his brand of horror is what Prawer terms 'unsafe,' where 'horror is brought, as Prawer puts it, into "our own world": the universe of apartment blocks, department stores and cafes' (Mazierska, 2007: 170). The resulting 'Polanskiesque style' is that 'radical combination of the absurd, the erotic, and the uncanny [taking] us to that place where nightmares become objects of desire' (Ehrenstein, 2012: 37), attesting to what Clover discerns, maintaining this fundamental train of thought and citing Tzvetan Todorov, who argued the 'very heart' of the fantastic is a world 'which is indeed our world, the one we know, a world without devils, sylphides, or vampires,' and it is here where an event can occur 'which cannot be explained by the laws of this same familiar world. The person who experiences the event'—and though a general statement, this essentially gets at the crux of what plagues *Repulsion*'s Carol—'must opt for one of two possible solutions: either he is the victim of an illusion of the senses, of a product of the imagination—and laws of the world then remain what they are; or else the event has indeed taken place, it is an integral part of reality—but then this reality is controlled by laws unknown to us' (Clover, 2015: 67).

'For Polanski,' Greenburg argues, 'existence has always carried a sense of dread' (2013: 83). Referencing *Rosemary's Baby* and *The Pianist*, the author contends that in all of Polanski's best films, ordinary people have their worst nightmares magnified, a recurring narrative and thematic refrain that forms part of a comprehensive Polanski worldview and follows a pattern regularly seen in more recent horror fare, where the universe of the contemporary horror film 'is an uncertain one in which good and evil, normality and abnormality, reality and illusion become virtually indistinguishable' (Prince, 2004: 85). As in the case of the safe haven, which is supposed to 'keep the killer out' and yet can quickly become, once the killer penetrates the fortress, 'the walls that hold the victim in' (Grant, 200: 79), these very surroundings, where Carol seeks refuge, are ultimately themselves reagents for anguish, making it so that there is never a truly protected space. It's a terrifying notion for an individual, and Polanski and Deneuve frighteningly convey the associative connotations of unlimited yet restricted dread, striking at the core of *Repulsion*'s unnerving terror, which maneuvers through what Pinedo calls the 'classical paradigm' in which 'the violent disruption is often located in or originates from a remote, exotic location.' 'In contrast,' she writes, 'the postmodern paradigm treats violence as a constituent element of everyday life' (Prince, 2004: 91). The house with all its trappings of security and positive solitude can indeed be just the opposite. It can be a claustrophobic setting where all is not right, where everyday realities and mundane customs surrender to not just external forces but, as in the case of *Repulsion*, something deeper and, apparently, unavoidable. Polanski, remarks Ehrenstein, 'sees the world through a prism that is dark, dislocated, and nightmarish' (2012: 37), and it's a perspective encapsulated and augmented by this often-foreboding single location.

Fig. 23. The horror of what anyone may be capable of.

What goads Polanski on, states Orr, 'is the sense that he can produce a supernatural delirium in his spectators, a form of delusion where they perceive action through the genre frame of horror to imagine the supernatural and stir up their wider fascination with extra-sensory perception' (Orr/Ostrowska, 2006: 10), which is part of what sets a film like *Repulsion* apart from its ilk, and is part of what defines Polanski's work in total. 'If *Repulsion* is about perceptual extremes it is also about emotional extremes' (Orr/Ostrowska, 2006: 12), Orr notes, and one is resultingly able to associate with the fantastic and unusual events of these films because of the strong bond with the respective protagonists, an ability to empathize even with that, or with who, is so unfamiliar, in part deriving precisely from our familiarity. It is very much a picture of *our* world and the elements that link *our* perceptions and *our* reactions to what is seen and what engages these characters that is 'essential to the modern horror film.' In Polanski's work, and *Repulsion* is arguably the preeminent case in point, the terror is less about 'the mere presence of a monster,' as Cosimo Urabno remarks, 'but a set of peculiar and specific feelings that the films elicit in their viewers' (Schneider, 2009: 25). Regardless of how inordinate certain situations may be, there is an incontestable connection that forms a considerable part of the horror genre's allure, certainly in the films from Polanski and certainly *Repulsion*, which Matty Stanfield calls 'one of the most intimately disturbing films ever made,' the intimacy emanating 'not only from the style in which it is crafted but also from a universally shared fear of losing grasp with our own perception of reality.' 'The film gradually pulls us into the protagonist's hysteria leaving the viewer disoriented and distressed,' so that by the time 'Polanski's grim little movie comes to its ambiguous ending and circular cinematic "logic," it is impossible to not relate to Catherine Deneuve's character' (2015). We have seen others looking at Carol (Colin is twice depicted attempting to get her attention through a partition of glass, an indication of the intrusion he will routinely encounter), and we have been made aware of a life existing apart from Carol (her coworker's social life; the images Polanski holds before and after Carol enters or exits the frame; the ominous phone calls Helen receives, presumably from Michael's wife), but by the end of the film, as the neighbors gather in and around Carol's apartment, gawking at what she hath wrought while her sister and Michael attempt to also make sense of the situation, we step outside Carol's madness to bear witness to the horror of others, a horror that presents the disconcerting notion of what anyone—anyone we know—may be capable of. It's a curious associative process that Polanski, better than most, could understand and illustrate, presenting unpleasant and disturbing events while remaining engaged all the same. Therefore, writes Laine, 'the disgust-horror that *Repulsion* evokes, is marked by its paralyzing and obsessive quality.

In comparison, in real life 'regular' disgust and fear are imperative emotions that direct our attention to relevant details in a dangerous situation. They also alert us to be on the lookout for more indications that are crucial for a closer assessment of the situation, and they encourage us to form expectations about how we should respond to a possible evolvement of the situation. This means that, unlike what is popularly believed, we are not merely passive victims of our emotions, but we often employ them in order to gain insight and knowledge that is especially meaningful and important to us (2011).

'An absolute masterpiece of psychological horror,' Repulsion, which no less an authority than George Romero named his favorite horror movie, 'ushered in, along with Hitchcock's Psycho and Powell's Peeping Tom, the modern day horror film' (Greco: 2019), extending its influence, alongside Polanski's other forays into horror, to the likes of David Cronenberg, who 'would literalize the idea of the human body as a space of confinement, a fear lurking under the surfaces of each film in the Apartment Trilogy.' But, comments, Wojtas, 'having knifed as deeply into the neurons of modernity as possible, Polanski himself simply opted out, leaving in his wake a map of the psyche's terrain that's all fissures' (Wojtas). The truth for Butler is that 'like any worthwhile film, Repulsion demands more than a single viewing,' with 'hardly a frame which has not a dual purpose—simultaneously developing and commenting on the story' (1972: 156), and it is, for Daniel Kurland, 'the film that should come to mind when "psychological thrillers and horror" are brought up' (2016). But how did Polanski ultimately view the film? When actor John Fraser asked the director if he'd been analyzed, because 'the film is sick,' Polanski simply responded, 'But, John, it's meant to be funny' (Sandford, 2008: 84). And in a 1995 estimation of the film, Polanski made his final case to Marc Weitzmann. 'Repulsion?' he mused, 'It's not disturbing at all' (Cronin, 2005: 155).

BIBLIOGRAPHY

Adams, Sam. 'So beautiful and yet so disordered.' *Los Angeles Times*, July 26, 2009 https://www.latimes.com/archives/la-xpm-2009-jul-26-ca-secondlook26-story.html

Baker, Emily-Rose. 'Sex and Psychosis: Roman Polanski's Repulsion and the Inherent Trauma of Womanhood.' *TrackChanges*, September 8, 2018. https://trackchangesjournal.wordpress.com/2018/09/08/sex-and-psychosis-roman-polanskis-repulsion-and-the-inherent-trauma-of-womanhood

Bradshaw, Peter. 'Repulsion.' *The Guardian*, January 3, 2013 https://www.theguardian.com/film/2013/jan/03/repulsion-review

Butler, Ivan. *The Cinema of Roman Polanski*. New York: A.S. Barnes & Co., 1970.

Butler, Ivan. *Horror in the Cinema*. New York: Warner, 1972.

Caputo, Davide. *Polanski and Perception: The Psychology of Seeing and the Cinema of Roman Polanski*. Bristol, UK: Intellect, 2012.

Clover, Carol J. *Men, Women, and Chainsaws: Gender in the Modern Horror Film*. Princeton: Princeton University Press, 2015.

Creed, Barbara. *The Monstrous-Feminine: Film, Feminism, Psychoanalysis*. London: Routledge, 2007.

Criterion Collection. *Repulsion* DVD Commentary 2009.

Cronin, Paul, ed. *Roman Polanski: Interviews*. Jackson: University of Mississippi, 2005.

Cwik, Greg. '50 years ago, Repulsion pioneered a new genre of gendered horror.' *AV Club*, October 31, 2015 https://film.avclub.com/50-years-ago-repulsion-pioneered-a-new-genre-of-gender-1798285951

Ehrenstein, David. *Masters of Cinema: Roman Polanski*. Paris: Phaidon, 2012.

Feeney, F.X. *Roman Polanski*. Koln: Taschen, 2006.

Grant, Barry Keith, ed. *The Dread of Difference: Gender and the Horror Film*. Austin: University of Texas Press, 2000.

Greco, John. 'Deneuve, Polanski, and Repulsion.' *Twenty Four Frames*, August 25, 2019 https://twentyfourframes.wordpress.com/2019/08/25/deneuve-polanski-and-repulsion.

Greenberg, James. *Roman Polanski: A Retrospective*. New York: Abrams, 2013.

Hagen, Kate. '31 Days of Feminist Horror Films: ROSEMARY'S BABY + REPULSION. *Medium*, October 11, 2016 https://blog.blcklst.com/31-days-of-feminist-horror-films-rosemarys-baby-repulsion-156ebb671c81.

Harrington, Erin. *Women, Monstrosity and Horror Film*: Gynehorror. London: Routledge, 2018.

Hendrix, Aaron. 'A Crack That Needs Mending: Roman Polanski's Repulsion.' *Talk Film Society* https://talkfilmsociety.com/articles/a-crack-that-needs-mending-roman-polanskis-repulsion?rq=polanski.

Holland, Norman. 'Roman Polanski, Repulsion, 1965.' *A Sharper Focus* http://www.asharperfocus.com/repulsio.htm.

Horrigan, Bill. 'Repulsion: Eye of the Storm.' Criterion Collection, July 27, 2009 https://www.criterion.com/current/posts/1207-repulsion-eye-of-the-storm.

Hutchings, Peter. *The Horror Film*. England: Pearson Education Limited, 2004.

Ipcar, Jenna. 'Repulsion at Catherine Deneuve and Roman Polanski.' *Back Row*, March 7, 2018 http://www.back-row.com/home/2018/3/7/repulsion-at-catherine-deneuve-and-roman-polanski.

Janisse, Kier-La. *House of Psychotic Women*. England: FAB Press Ltd., 2016.

Kiernan, Thomas. *Roman Polanski: A Biography*. New York: Grove Press, 1980.

Kiernan, Thomas. *The Roman Polanski Story*. New York: Grove Press, 1980.

Kristeva, Julia. *Powers of Horror: An Essay on Abjection*. New York: Columbia University Press, 1982.

Kurland, Daniel. 'Roman Polanski's Psychological Horror Tour-De-Force, 'Repulsion', Turns 51!' *Bloody Disgusting*, October 3, 2016 https://bloody-disgusting.com/movie/3408569/roman-polanskis-psychological-horror-tour-de-force-repulsion-turns-51.

Laine, Tarja. 'Imprisoned in Disgust: Roman Polanski's Repulsion.' *Film-Philosophy*, February 15, 2011.

Leaming, Barbara. *Polanski: A Biography. The Filmmaker as Voyeur.* New York: Simon and Schuster, 1981.

Macintyre, Elaine. 'Repulsion Film Review.' *Cult Classics* http://www.elainemacintyre.net/film_reviews/repulsion.php.

Mazierska, Ewa. *Roman Polanski: The Cinema of a Cultural Traveler.* London: I.B. Tauris, 2007.

Meikle, Denis. *Roman Polanski: The Horror Films.* England: Hemlock Books, 2016.

Meikle, Denis. *Roman Polanski: Odd Man Out.* London: Reynolds & Hearn Ltd, 2006.

Moore, Elise. 'Sexual Violence and Female Experience in Roman Polanski's Apartment Trilogy: Repulsion, Rosemary's Baby, The Tenant.' *Bright Lights Film Journal*, June 6, 2016 https://brightlightsfilm.com/sexual-violence-female-experience-roman-polanskis-apartment-trilogy-repulsion-rosemarys-baby-tenant/#.Xf50p_x7mUk.

Morgan, Kim. 'Roman Polanski Understands Women: Repulsion.' *Huffington Post*, December 6, 2017 https://www.huffpost.com/entry/roman-polanski-understand_b_301292.

Morrison, James. *Roman Polanski: Contemporary Film Directors.* Urbana: University of Illinois Press, 2007.

Orr, John and Elzbieta Ostrowska, eds. *The Cinema of Roman Polanski: Dark Spaces of the World.* London and New York: Wallflower Press, 2006.

Polanski, Roman. *Roman.* New York: Ballantine, 1985.

Prince, Stephen, ed. *The Horror Film.* New Jersey: Rutgers University Press, 2004.

Sandford, Christopher. *Polanski: A Biography.* New York: Palgrave Macmillan, 2008.

Schneider, Steven Jay. *Horror Film and Psychoanalysis: Freud's Worst Nightmare.* Cambridge: Cambridge University Press, 2009.

Stanfield, Matty. 'The Cracks That Can't Be Mended or Polanski's Repulsion.' *MattyStanfield.com*. October 22, 2015. https://mattystanfield.com/2015/10/21/the-cracks-that-cant-be-mended-or-polanskis-repulsion.

Truffot, Didier. 'The Eye Boundary: Repulsion.' *Senses of Cinema*, March 2018 http://sensesofcinema.com/2018/cteq/the-eye-boundary-repulsion.

Wojtas, Michael. 'The keys to Polanski's Apartment Trilogy & Rosemary's Baby.' *Impose Magazine* https://www.imposemagazine.com/bytes/chatter/the-keys-to-polanskis-apartment-trilogy-rosemarys-baby.

Worland, Rick. *The Horror Film: An Introduction*. Massachusetts: Blackwell Publishing, 2007.

DEVIL'S ADVOCATES

"Auteur Publishing's new Devil's Advocates critiques on individual titles offer bracingly fresh perspectives from passionate writers. The series will perfectly complement the BFI archive volumes." Christopher Fowler, Independent on Sunday

THE BLOOD ON SATAN'S CLAW – DAVID EVANS-POWELL

"Evans-Powell has written a powerful and fascinating monograph that is very readable. ...always feels relevant and interesting." Folk Horror Revival

MACBETH – REBEKAH OWENS

"Rebekah Owens argues that the film is a powerful and innovative horror classic. ...this is an instructive read..." Shakespeare Magazine

WITCHFINDER GENERAL – IAN COOPER

"Cooper writes with clarity, wit and confidence, his obvious fondness for the film and for movies in general evident throughout... I enjoyed it so much that I read the book in one sitting, then returned to scour it for any details I might have missed." Horror Talk